Ingenious ABE

Ingenious ABE

STORIES FROM THE LIFE OF ABRAHAM LINCOLN

Written by Ron L. Andersen

Illustrated by Jay Fontano

Plain Sight Publishing
An Imprint of Cedar Fort, Inc.
Springville, Utah

ISBN 13: 978-1-4621-1789-5

Published by Plain Sight Publishing, an imprint of
Cedar Fort, Inc., 2373 W. 700 S., Springville, UT 84663
Distributed by Cedar Fort, Inc., www.cedarfort.com

Library of Congress Control Number: 2015954716

Cover design by Lauren Error

Edited and typeset by Deborah Spencer

Printed in the United States of America

10 9 8 7 6 5 4 3 2 1

Printed on acid-free paper

Dedication

To our grandchildren—treasures from heaven

Other books by Ron L. Andersen:

Abraham Lincoln—God's Humble Instrument
Abraham Lincoln and Joseph Smith

Contents

Introduction 1
Chapter One: "Thar's Suthin' Peculiarsome 'bout Abe" 3
Chapter Two: A Piece of Floating Driftwood 12
Chapter Three: "Some Legal Rights Are Moral Wrongs" . . . 24
Chapter Four: Mary Todd 30
Chapter Five: Congressman Lincoln 37
Chapter Six: What Was He Thinking? 44
Chapter Seven: The Unlikely President 51
Chapter Eight: Off to Washington 60
Chapter Nine: I, Abraham Lincoln, Do Solemnly Swear . . . 65
Chapter Ten: A New Birth of Freedom 77
Chapter Eleven: "Now He Belongs to the Ages" 86
Endnotes 93
Sources 98
About the Author 100
About the Illustrator 101

Introduction

Some people are destined to change the world, but they often come in unexpected packages. You may picture Superman, Spider-man, or Captain America dressed up in their super suits. In reality everyday heroes don't dress up like that. They don't fight goblins, monsters, or aliens. They may wear a top hat or even be clumsy. Everyday heroes are everyday people who find a purpose they are willing to fight for.

Abraham Lincoln, the sixteenth president of the United States, was one of these everyday heroes. He didn't have money, formal education, or even experience in leading people. He had no rich or influential family members to get him to the top of the political ladder. But he never let hard things stop him from accomplishing his goals. Abraham Lincoln had the drive to make a positive difference in everything he did. He was kind, proactive, inventive, and clever. Some would even call him ingenious.

This is the story of Ingenious Abe, a man unmatched among our most honored American heroes.

Chapter One

"Thar's Suthin' Peculiarsome 'bout Abe"[1]

Abe Lincoln was no stranger to death. And he hated it. He was seven years old when his family said their last good-bye to baby Thomas, lying in his lonely grave in Redmon Cemetery in Kentucky. With tearful waves they rolled away in a wagon filled with their belongings to begin a new life in southern Indiana, a state free from slavery, but not free from more death, hardships, and trials.

If the young Lincoln family hoped for an easier way of life in Indiana, they were quickly disappointed. Their new homestead was so deep in an unbroken forest that Abe and his father had to hack out a path to get their family to their new home. Already sweaty and exhausted, Thomas, Abe's father, had to build a shelter for his family. Though he probably had great dreams to construct something beautiful, the best he could offer them was three walls, a roof, and a dirt floor. He left the fourth side open to the elements and kept a fire burning day and night. Their home was a wild and lonely place for his small family. The closest potential friends lived one to two miles away.

Ironically, tragedy and challenges season heroes. Abe,

this everyday hero, was no different as he mourned the death of his dear mother to an illness called milk sickness. The sickness came from a poisonous white snakeroot plant that the cows ate. Living in nineteenth-century America wasn't easy. Modern medicine was not available. For days Nancy's life dwindled, and she knew she was going to die. Before she took her last breath, she gathered Abe and his older sister, Sarah, to her bedside and asked them to be kind to their father, one another, and the world. She encouraged them to love God and their fellow men.[2]

On October 5, 1818, Nancy, "one of the very best women in the whole race,"[3] was buried on a wooded knoll. Before the age of ten, Abe had buried his younger brother and dear mother. If life was fair, death should have spared Abe of any more visits, but Abe would also lose his only sister, Sarah, and two adored sons to death's relentless sting. These early experiences of grief and sadness taught Abe compassion that enabled him to make a difference in people's lives.

Even though Dennis Hank, their fun-loving relative, did his best to help the Lincolns, Thomas could see that his children were faring poorly in the absence of their mother. Their cabin and the children were dirty and disorderly without her caring influence. They all missed her terribly. So thirteen months after Nancy's death, on a cold November day, Thomas struck out for Kentucky, traveling on lonely roads, crossing the Ohio River to Elizabethtown with the hope of returning home with a wife.

Answering an unexpected knock on the door, the young widow, Sarah Bush Johnston, with her three fatherless children, was surprised to see her old childhood friend, Thomas Lincoln. She had not him seen for years.

But what he had to say was even more startling to her.

Thomas wasted no time in explaining his purpose to Sarah. He said, "I have no wife and you have no husband. I came a-purpose to marry you. I knowed you from a gal and you knowed me from a boy. I've no time to lose; and if you're willin' let it be done straight off."[4]

How startled Sarah must have been to receive such an unexpected and abrupt marriage proposal! After thinking quietly for a few moments, she gave her answer. "I got a few little debts."[5] She made him a list of people she owed money to and together they paid them. They were married December 2, 1819.

Sarah Bush Lincoln's arrival marked a turning point in the life of the young and grieving Abe. She brought with her a new level of civilization. She brought bedding, furniture, and silverware to fill their empty kitchen space. The Lincoln children had never known such luxury.

Sarah also brought her children, Elizabeth, John D., and Matilda, whose ages ranged from thirteen to eight years old. Sarah's children revived the miserable Lincoln children, and Sarah transformed the Lincoln home with her love and light. She kissed and cleaned up the dirty faces, washed the clothes of the Lincoln children, and added more meat to frail frames. She intended to make them look "more human."

The Lincoln cabin didn't escape Abe's new stepmother's remodeling. Thomas and Dennis made a floor for the cabin, finished the roof, added a proper door, and created a window covered in grease paper. Sarah installed three beds in the loft for Dennis Hanks, Abe, and John. Despite the amount of work the family had to put in, they all loved the changes.

What was even more extraordinary, Sarah Bush Lincoln was able to blend the two families harmoniously and without jealousy. She loved Sarah and Abe just as she loved her own children. Yet she grew especially fond of Abraham. "I never gave him a cross word in all my life. . . . His mind and mine seemed to move together—move in the same channel." Many years later, when asked to compare her son and her stepson, she told an interviewer, "Both were good boys, but I must say . . . that Abe was the best boy I ever saw or ever expect to see."[6]

Starved for a mother's affection, Abe returned her love. He called her Mama and always spoke to her with love and respect. Sarah wanted Abe and his sister to remember their mother and suggested that they all refer to her as their angel mother. Abe liked that.

Sarah and Thomas Lincoln could not read or write but did what she could to educate their children. Abe was only able to attend school occasionally although he wished he could attend every session. He loved to learn but only completed about one year of education in a school. Abe's new mother described him as being driven to master all that he read and heard. "He must understand everything—even to the smallest thing—minutely and exactly. He would repeat it over and over to himself again and again . . . and when it was fixed in his mind to suit him he . . . never lost that fact or his understanding of it."[7]

Before long, adult neighbors in the area would seek Abe out to write letters for them that they could not write themselves. He was always glad to do it.

Dennis Hanks remembered, "Abe was getting hungry for book[s], reading everything he could get his hands on."[8] He took books with him to the fields to read during

rest periods. When he returned, Dennis recalled, "he would routinely go to the cupboard, snatch a piece of cornbread, pick up a book, sit down in a chair, cock his legs up as high as his head, and read."[9]

Abe didn't have many books, but his two favorite books were the Bible and *Aesop's Fables* and he read them often.

Abe loved to write but he rarely had a pencil and paper. So he would scrawl his words on a shovel or a board with charcoal. Or he would shape them in dirt, sand, or snow with a stick. His youthful fascination with writing and reading served him well years later when he became president.

Sometimes Dennis would help Abe make ink from blackberry briar root, and Abe learned to fashion pens from a turkey buzzard feather.

When Abe wrote his name, he would say, "Denny look at that, will you? *Abraham Lincoln!* That stands fur me. Don't look a blamed bit like me!"[10]

"He'd stand and study it a spell," wrote Dennis. " 'Peared to mean a heap to Abe."[11] "Aunt Sairy never let the children pester him. She always said Abe was goin' to be a great man some day. An' she wasn't goin' to have him hindered."[12]

Sarah Bush Lincoln remembered, "He was the best boy I ever saw. He never told me a lie in his life, never evaded, never quarreled, never dodged nor turned a corner to avoid any chastisement or other responsibility. He never swore or used profane language in my presence nor in others' that I remember of . . . He loved children well, very well."[13]

Abe was always taller than other children his age.

He wore a coonskin cap, buckskin breeches, and moccasins to school. "The way we all dressed them days,"[14] Dennis recalled. They had no boots for winter snow so they strapped birch bark with hickory bark soles under their yarn socks as a snow shoe.[15] Most school sessions were held during winter months, so in this fashion the Lincoln children would walk up to four miles to attend.

One classmate remembered, "There was bare and naked six or more inches of Abe Lincoln's shin bone."[16]

Despite this unique fashion statement, Abe seemed to care little about his peculiar appearance. Wherever he was, he would draw the other children to him as he told them stories, cracked jokes, and made them laugh with delight. Almost from the beginning he took his place as leader. He was a friend to everyone. Yet through it all, it was frequently noted that Abe, in sharp contrast to other men and boys on the frontier, did not swear, smoke or chew tobacco, or drink whiskey. Neither did he view blacks or Indians as inferior to whites like many did in that day.

In the evenings, farm boys would gather at the Gentryville store hoping that Abe would be there. When he was, he would entertain them for hours. But many times he wasn't and they would complain that Abe was at home always diggin' into books.

"Thar's suthin' peculiarsome about Abe,"[17] Dennis Hanks said. "It seemed that Abe made books tell him more than they told other people."[18]

The other farm boys had gone to school and read *The Kentucky Preceptor*, but Abe would ask his friends deep questions like, "Who has the most right to complain, the Indian or the Negroes?" Then he would talk about it for hours while he worked with them in the cornfields.

Once hearing that court would be in session in nearby Boonville, Indiana, Abe walked the fifteen miles to watch the proceedings. He observed every detail with rapt interest as the lawyers methodically worked their cases to the juries. Abe wanted to do something with his life outside of working the land on the frontier, but he didn't know how that would ever be possible.

By age sixteen, Abe towered over other youth his age at six feet two inches. He was a skinny but strong. His family depended on him more and more for his share of the farm work, but his mind was always on his books.

A friend remarked, "He said to me one day that his father taught him to work, but he never taught him to love it."[19]

In the evenings, Abe and his father would spend hours telling and retelling stories and jokes. Dennis Hanks said that Thomas Lincoln was the only one better than Abe at telling stories and cracking jokes. Above all, Abe was remembered by fellow settlers for his kindness, his sense of fair play, his helpfulness to others, and his love for animals. All saw and admired Abe's determination to do much more with his life than so many of those around him.

Abe was remarkably strong and would not back away from a friendly challenge of strength. At eighteen, he would amaze his friends by taking a large and heavy ax at the end of the handle and hold it out from his shoulders in a straight horizontal line, easy and steady. His friends would try to duplicate the feat but none of them could do it. Years later, while president in his fifties, Abe was vigorously chopping wood with some soldiers. He repeated this feat of holding the ax parallel to the ground nice and steady to the amazement of the much younger men who were unable to match his strength.

Chapter Two

A Piece of Floating Driftwood

Abe itched for something more than becoming a landowner and farmer. But there were few opportunities in that region of frontier America. He and Dennis Hanks decided to sell firewood to the steamers on the Ohio River to put a few coins in their penniless pockets, only to find the demand slack and money scarce. But it was the lure of the river that gave Abraham his first glimpse of escape from the confinement of frontier life. He jumped at an offer to take a flatboat of goods to New Orleans for eight dollars a month. He relished the adventure of the thousand-mile float down the mighty Mississippi River. New Orleans, with its forty thousand residents, was the first city Abe had ever visited. He marveled at the large buildings, the markets, and the sailing ships at port in the bustling city.

It was in New Orleans that he first encountered slaves in large numbers and the harsh reality of slavery's inhumanity. Slavery was a thriving business in America for 250 years. Some merchants purchased captured slaves in West Africa and shipped them to America to be sold for a profit. Others bought and sold slaves to plantation owners as if they were buying and selling cattle. The plantation owners purchased them to do the work in their fields. Nearly all in the slave business became rich. All that is, except the slaves themselves. Slaves were never paid for their work and were treated badly by the slave owners.

While in New Orleans Abe would have undoubtedly seen advertisements such as this:

"For sale—several likely girls from 10 to 18 years old, a woman 24, a very valuable woman 25, with three very likely children."[1]

Abe was horrified at the terrible treatment of these men, women, and children. He later told friends of his New Orleans experience, "Slavery ran the iron into me then and there."[2]

Upon his return to his family in Illinois, he dutifully handed his earned salary over to his father.

In March 1830, Abe helped his father and stepmother move to Macon County in central Illinois. Another outbreak of the milk sickness surfaced again in Indiana and Thomas wasn't about to have any more of that. He sold the place and headed north and west. By this time, at age twenty-one, Abe was old enough to strike out on his own and to vote at elections.

Their first winter in Illinois was disastrous, with snow falling to several feet deep, below zero temperatures, and dying livestock. This was followed by a devastating runoff in spring that ultimately convinced Thomas to make yet another move. This move did not include his son. Abe had other plans and was ready to build his own life with only one thing certain in his mind—his future would not include farming.

***

At age twenty-two, Abe and two friends were hired to build a flatboat. They loaded it with barrels of bacon, corn, wheat, and live hogs. They were to guide it, once again, to New Orleans. It was at the beginning of this second trip to Louisiana that marveling spectators saw Abe's ingenuity. The flatboat launched on the Sangamon River in central Illinois, headed for the Mississippi River. On the way it became stuck on the sawmill dam at the village of New Salem and began flooding. Abe and his friends furiously labored to free the boat and avoid losing their cargo. Before long, many in the village arrived to observe the spectacle. They watched as the tall Abe with his boots, hat, coat and vest thrown off, struggled unsuccessfully to free the craft.

As Abe bore a hole in the bow, or front of the boat, he directed his friends to move the cargo to the rear. His strange operation puzzled the New Salem villagers, but they soon saw that this procedure caused the stern, or back of the flatboat, to rise. When the water poured out through the hole that he bored, the whole craft slowly lifted and floated over the dam. The townsfolk were impressed at Abe's ingenuity, as was the relieved owner of the flatboat and cargo, Denton Offutt, who made plans then and there to hire the innovative Abe Lincoln upon his return from New Orleans.

Young Abe was enthralled again with the bustling city of New Orleans, except for the numerous slave pens. Slaves waited like animals in these high-walled enclosures for their dreaded day at the slave auction. They were

displayed and inspected with the intent of being sold to the highest bidder. Again Abe watched in horror as families were systematically disassembled—mothers being sold to one plantation owner, fathers to another, and children to still another. It was a heart-wrenching scene as these families anguished over their cruel separation.

Abe could not help but notice that the white auctioneers and buyers seemed unaffected by the awful scene. Leaning over to his companions he said, "Let's get away from this. If ever I get the opportunity to hit that thing [slavery] I'm going to hit it hard."[3] Little did he know that some four decades later, Abe would find himself at the head of this nation in civil war. It would be during this harrowing time that he would land the blow that would end slavery forever in the United States.

Like a "piece of floating driftwood,"[4] as he referred to himself at that time, he headed back to New Salem. It was the largest community Lincoln had ever resided in. He hired on with hard-drinking Denton Offutt for twelve dollars a month to cut down trees for the local sawmill. After a month of observing Abe's intellect, honesty, and sobriety, Offutt would hire him to clerk in his store.

Offutt would tell his tavern friends that Abe "knows more than anyone else in the United States."[5] He boasted of Abe's uncommon strength and prowess as an athlete. He would set up wagers or bets that Abe could out-wrestle anyone, even Jack Armstrong, the Clary's Grove champion wrestler. Abe did not like fighting, but he was not afraid of a good-natured contest. He also knew that the Clary boys could be more trouble to him if he did not come forth as a man and establish himself in the new community. So he agreed to challenge the Clary's Grove champion. Men came from miles around to view the match at Offutt's store.

"They pawed and clutched in many holds and twists till Lincoln threw Armstrong and had both shoulders to the grass," at which time Armstrong's gang started toward Lincoln with shouts and threats. Abe stepped to the store wall and defiantly told the angry gang that he would, "fight, race, or wrestle any who wanted to try him."[6] Jack Armstrong suddenly broke through the crowd and gripped Abe's hand, silenced them, and said that Lincoln was "fair" and "the best feller that ever broke into this settlement."[7] The two became best of friends.

Some days after the match, the Clary's Grove boys wanted to "see what stuff Abe Lincoln had in him."[8] So they rode into New Salem, sought out their target, and issued him a series of challenges. First, he was to wrestle a man from Little Grove. "All right," Abe said and nodded.[9] Second, he was to run a foot race against a running champion from the nearby community of Wolf. Abe coolly responded, "Trot him out."[10] And finally they demanded that he fight a man from Sand Ridge. "Nothing wrong about that," Abe replied.[11]

Abe ran faster than the champion from Wolf and bested the man from Sand Ridge. In the match with the man from Little Grove, Abe caught him by the nape of the neck and threw him out of the ring. Following this match, the gang approached him and said, "We will take you into our crowd."[12]

Abe welcomed their friendship and they liked him. Even with this acceptance into their gang, Abe would not join them in their mischief and drinking. Nor would he gamble with them. But he would, when asked, judge their horse races and cockfights, umpire their wrestling matches, and settle their disputes.

That summer, after years of delivering mimicked speeches and sermons to friends, Abe jumped at his first opportunity to deliver a real speech. He had heard that two state legislative candidates were to speak in Decatur. Abe made the journey and when the opportunity presented itself, he stepped forward and gave a speech on the need for improvement of the nearby Sangamon River for better navigation. He was glad to take part and express his opinion. And it planted a seed: he wanted more of this in his life.

Abe relished every opportunity to strike up conversation with everyone, with the exception of young ladies. He was painfully shy around them.

A New Salem resident recorded, "Lincoln was the strongest man I ever knew. And while Lincoln was full of fun and life, I never saw him dance and he courted no girls."[13]

Abe seemed more self-conscious of his appearance than he needed to be. He would often joke about it. Years later during a political debate with Stephen A. Douglas, Douglas angrily accused Lincoln of being two-faced. But rather than get angry at the insult he calmly joked to the crowd that if he had two faces, did they really think he would choose to wear this one? This invoked uproarious laughter from the audience.

Abe loved to tell this story.

> One day . . . I got into a fit of musing in my room and stood resting my elbows on the bureau. Looking into the glass, it struck me what an ugly man I was. The fact grew on me and I made up my mind that I

> must be the ugliest man in the world. It so maddened me that I resolved, should I ever see an uglier, I would shoot him on sight. Not long after this, Andy [naming a lawyer present] came to town and the first time I saw him I said to myself: "There's the man." I went home, took down my gun, and prowled around the streets waiting for him. He soon came along.
>
> "Halt, Andy," said I, pointing the gun at him, "say your prayers, for I am going to shoot you."
>
> "Why, Mr. Lincoln, what's the matter? What have I done?"
>
> "Well, I made an oath that if I ever saw an uglier man than I am, I'd shoot him on the spot. You are uglier, surely; so make ready to die."
>
> "Mr. Lincoln, do you really think that I am uglier than you?"
>
> "Yes."
>
> "Well, Mr. Lincoln," said Andy deliberately and looking me squarely in the face, "if I am any uglier, fire away."[14]

Abe was so entertaining that at times an entire neighborhood would gather just to hear him tell stories.

During his New Salem years, Abe was always looking to do a kindness or watching out for the underdog. He was strong but not a bully—apparently free from bad habits—and was known to be generous and sympathetic. It was widely told in the settlement of the time Abe had mistakenly overcharged a woman a few pennies and upon discovering his error, walked six miles to her home to return the overpaid change. Another time he used the wrong measure to weigh an order of tea, and again upon realization of his mistake, he walked the miles to the woman's home to deliver the rest of her order. Both of these errors could have been corrected upon the return of these customers to his store, but he could not wait. Upon discovering the errors, he closed his store and struck out to pay them their due. These astonished customers eagerly spoke of Abe's kind gestures to their neighbors.

The schoolmaster recorded, "He was among the best clerks I ever saw, he was attentive to his business—was kind and considerate to his customers and friends and always treated them with great tenderness—kindness and honesty."[15]

Business was slow at the store, leaving time for Abe to quench his thirst for books. "My best friend," he once said, "is the man who'll get me a book I ain't read."[16] He had little interest in fiction; what he loved to read was poetry, history, and biographies. When he heard that a farmer six miles away had Samuel Kirkham's *English Grammar,* he walked to his place to borrow the book, studied it cover to cover, and returned it.

Such stories circulated among his New Salem neighbors who marveled at the young, gangly bachelor who would not gamble, drink alcohol, or smoke or chew tobacco, yet was so friendly and sociable.

It was at this time in his young life that prominent men in the community recognized young Abe's unique intelligence and integrity. To his great surprise, they encouraged him to run for a seat in the Illinois state legislature. He was stunned at their suggestion, but he could not ignore the yearnings inside of him. Yes, this would be an opportunity to do good, to help others, to make the world around him a better place. Yes, he wanted this.

But how was he, a young man in his early twenties,

to know how to run for political office? He had no idea. But that did not stop him. What he did not know, he would find out. So with youthful enthusiasm, he asked questions, lots of questions, and listened intently to the advice of those with more experience than he about how he might accomplish this goal.

One thing he was sure of—he would not run this or any future campaign by criticizing his opponents or their opinions. He would run on his burning desire to serve others and make circumstances better for everyone. His primary political attribute would not be his experience, and it would not be his position in society. He had neither of these. It would be based upon his integrity and diligence. Having reached this conclusion, he wrote a simple political handbill for his first political pursuit.

He wrote, "Every man is said to have his peculiar ambition. Whether it be true or not, I can say, for one, that I have no other so great as that of being truly esteemed of my fellow-men by rendering myself worthy of their esteem."[17]

Despite his popularity in New Salem, Abe awoke on the morning of August 7, 1832, to learn that he had been defeated in his first run for a seat in the legislature. In the surrounding county, where he was relatively unknown, few people voted for him. But in the precinct that included New Salem, the vote for him was nearly unanimous. The fire was kindled inside of him. He would run in the next race in 1834.

As early as 1832, Abe, with his exceptional self-education, was drawing up legal documents for his newfound friends. He was not yet a lawyer at that time, but even before coming to New Salem he had studied law books. He even appeared from time to time in court to plead a case. He owned a book of legal forms that he used to write up deeds, mortgages, and other documents for those who needed them. He rarely charged any fees even though he desperately needed the income.

Abe was intensely interested in law and yearned for what appeared to be the impossible—the opportunity to become a lawyer. Attendance at law school required money or influential family or friends, and Abe had neither. This dream seemed unreachable, yet he took every opportunity to move himself closer to his dream. On occasion, he borrowed a law book from local lawyers. These he studied from cover to cover before returning them.

But to fully understand law and gain a license to become a lawyer, he would need what was commonly referred to as Blackstone's Commentaries, or *Commentaries on the Laws of England* by William Blackstone. These books contained the founding principles upon which United States law was based, and these books were not available to him in New Salem.

Remarkably and to his utter surprise, Abe acquired these needed texts in a most unexpected way. A stranger migrating west purchased some supplies from Abe's store. The stranger didn't have enough room in his wagon for the new items, so he took an old barrel from the wagon and asked Abe if he would buy it. Abe made a passing inspection of the contents of the barrel and determined that it contained little of value to him but he obliged him anyway by paying half a dollar for the barrel. The barrel sat in his store for days before he emptied all of the contents. When he did, he discovered a set of Blackstone's *Commentaries* at the bottom of the barrel. These books would be the keys to Abe's future.

Even with the books, he could not afford to attend a law school, but he would not be denied. He resolved to teach himself. He immersed himself in the law books with his usual intensity, later declaring that never in his life was his mind so thoroughly absorbed.

A local resident recalled, "His favorite place to study was a wooded knoll near New Salem, where he threw himself under a wide-spreading oak, and expansively made a reading desk of the hillside. Here he would pour over *Blackstone* day after day, shifting his position as the sun rose and sank, so as to keep in the shade."[18]

Abe was so absorbed in his studies that people would walk by and their friendly hellos received only silence. But his obsession with learning law paid off. Judge Bowling Green took an interest in young Abe's determination and would talk with him about Illinois law. He even allowed Abe to try small cases without a fee, examine witnesses, and make arguments under his supervision in his courtroom.

Chapter Three

"Some Legal Rights Are Moral Wrongs"[1]

In the midst of Abe's financial difficulties, he was eager to make a second and more determined run for the state legislature in 1834. Again his friends were ready to support him. In this campaign, he made fewer statements on political issues but chose rather to approach it by riding throughout the county to meet face to face with the residents. Many more people knew him through surveying jobs he had done, and he had gained a reputation for accuracy and fairness.

On one occasion he approached a field where some thirty men were at work harvesting grain. He began speaking to the workers when one of them grumbled that he would cast no vote for any man that could not hold his own in the field.

Abe replied, "Well, boys if that is all, I am sure of your votes."[2] He then grabbed a harvesting cradle and with perfect ease led the harvesters on a full round of the field. The workers were pleased with his hard work and nearly all decided then and there to cast their vote for Abe.

The votes were cast on August 4 in which the top four would be elected. At age twenty-five, Abe was elected to

the Illinois state legislature. He was grateful that so many people in the county supported him in the campaign. Abe borrowed money from a friend to purchase the first suit he had ever owned so he could make a decent appearance in the legislature. This was an important purchase because the long, lanky bachelor did not often impress with his appearance.

During the six-week legislative session, Abe's fellow legislators noticed his superior writing ability and many asked him to write up bills that they would sponsor. Of course he gladly accepted. It didn't take long for them to observe that this good-natured newcomer from New Salem seemed always to be ready for a good laugh.

***

If there ever was a young man that needed the companionship and influence of a woman, it was Abe Lincoln. With all of his ease around people in general, around young women he was painfully shy and clumsy. He would avoid waiting on young women in his store if he could, allowing his partner to attend them. Abe was probably painfully conscious of his appearance and did not have the means or the know-how to do much about it. He needed someone to cook for him and clean and repair his tattered clothes, which meant nearly all of them, minus his new legislative suit. His clothes rarely ever fit him. He was just too tall.

Abe's first love interest, Ann Rutledge, tragically died, probably from typhoid. He drowned himself again in his studies, which helped him manage his grief and loneliness over Ann's passing. Approximately a year after Ann's death, on September 9, 1836, Abe held a license in his hands that authorized him to practice law in the Illinois courts.

Abe ran again for the same office in 1836 and garnered more votes than any of the seventeen candidates. His peers in the minority **Whig Party** elected him as Floor Leader for their political party in the legislature.

In a session of the state legislature, Abe was troubled when his fellow legislators voted to support slavery in their state. For some years, the Southern states had been growing more angry over the rising antislavery feelings in the North. Strong signs of a divided nation were becoming evident as early as the 1830s.

Whig Party: The Whig Party stood strong against slavery and in favor of economic development through river and road improvements. It was the beginning framework for the Republican Party.

Twenty-eight-year-old Abe listened intently as the legislature heard the resolution. He was saddened at the discriminatory feelings of the majority of his friends in the legislature. As the Speaker of the House was preparing to call for a vote, Abe was faced with a challenging dilemma. If he voted against the resolution to support slavery, he might be the only one. This could make things difficult for him in the future. What would the other legislators think of him for being so different from the rest?

The Speaker called for a vote, and in alphabetical order the clerk called each legislator by name to cast his vote.

When the clerk came to the name of Assemblyman Lincoln the vote stood 32 Ayes, and 0 Nays. No one in that room could possibly know that the next man to vote would be the sixteenth president of the United States. It would be Abe Lincoln who would end two and one half centuries of slavery.

The clerk called, "Mr. Lincoln?"

And the assembly hall rang out with a resounding, "Nay!"

And so began Abe's assault on slavery in America. Just as he suspected, the other legislators shifted in their seats and raised their eyebrows in surprise. The young and inexperienced Abe, only days into this term in the legislature, had just voted against his friends who had cast their votes.

Abe was pleased that five others would follow his courageous leadership with a nay vote. But as expected, the ending votes were 77 to 6. The resolution was forwarded to the Senate where it was passed unanimously—not a single dissenting vote.

But Abe did not give up. He and fellow opponent Dan Stone recorded a formal protest in the legislature that stated their opposition to slavery in their state.

At the conclusion of the legislative session, Abe returned to what was left of his beloved New Salem to say good-bye. He would be compelled to move on.

Abe arrived in his new home of Springfield riding a borrowed horse and carrying all that he owned in two small saddlebags. Not an impressive sight. While other men at this stage of life had married or owned farms or businesses, he was still poor and owned nothing. The respected lawyer and future US senator John Todd Stuart had invited the bachelor to be his law partner in Springfield. Stuart was a cousin to Abe's future wife, Mary Todd.

The law firm of Stuart and Lincoln was busy with cases, and Abe was gaining valuable experience. He was prone to help the poorer citizens, not really caring that they had little to pay him. He just wanted to help them.

His fellow lawyers would say that Abe's problem of not earning a comfortable living was his own fault because he continued to place the interests of others above his own.

Abe often said, "Some legal rights are moral wrongs."[3] By this he meant that people can sometimes use the law to gain an unfair advantage over another person. He went on for his entire legal and political career to demonstrate that he would go to great lengths to avoid a moral wrong or injury to other persons. This often resulted in lost income opportunities for himself and some occasional ridicule. But he didn't seem to mind.

Chapter Four

Mary Todd

Mary Todd was the belle of the town and captured the interest of nearly every eligible bachelor, including Abe. The daughter of a prosperous Kentucky banker and merchant, Mary had grown up with the best that money could buy. She was carefully attended by family slaves and educated in the best private schools. She was described as having light chestnut hair, beautiful soft skin, and stunning blue eyes. She was witty, dignified, graceful, and a charming conversationalist. She also had a sharp tongue.

When Abe met her at a party at a mansion in Springfield, he told her that he wanted to dance with her "in the worst way."[1] Mary laughed and they danced. After the dance she teasingly told her clumsy suitor that he had certainly danced in the worst way. The intelligent and vivacious Mary Todd enchanted Abe, and somehow he impressed her. With her, he was completely comfortable and they would talk for hours. Interested in politics, she admired his ambition and integrity. She was known to have said that she would marry a man who would someday be president. By Christmas of 1840, Mary and Abraham were engaged.

Shortly after the happy announcement, Abe wavered. He worried about his ability to earn enough money to make Mary or any wife happy. He owned no home, had no savings, and had only a few possessions. But what hurt him most was the fact that her family did not approve of him as a suitable match for Mary. Abe told Mary that he did not love her, though he really did. They broke off the engagement and, by so doing, broke Mary's heart and his.

Instead of feeling relieved, Abe was devastated. He was so deeply unhappy and depressed that he did not leave his room for a week. He told his best friend, Joshua Speed, that he was haunted by "the never-absent idea"[2] that he had made Mary unhappy. "That still kills my soul. I can not but reproach myself, for even wishing to be happy while she is otherwise."[3]

He told Mary's cousin John Todd Stuart that "I am now the most miserable man living."[4]

Simeon Francis, a newspaper editor, and his wife, Eliza took a liking to Abe. They treated him much like a member of their family. They were both saddened at the breakup of Abe and Mary and more particularly the reasons for the separation. Abe and Mary entered 1842 just as they had the previous year, not seeing or speaking to one another. That condition remained unchanged until midyear when Eliza Francis determined to do something about it.

Mrs. Francis invited Mary to their home for a visit and did the same to Abe. But they didn't tell Mary that they had invited Abe or Abe that they had invited Mary. The two unwittingly complied and found the surprise of their lives when Mrs. Francis marched Abe into a room where the unsuspecting Mary was sitting. The two stunned lovers gazed at each other, speechless and bewildered, for the first time in a year and a half.

Mrs. Francis placed Mary's hand into the large rough hand of the dumbfounded Abe and flatly told them, "Be friends again."[5] Then she walked out of the room and closed the door.

And they did. This unsuspected reunion sparked the embers of love in both of them and rekindled their affection for each other. After several more months of rebuilding their tender feelings for each other, Abe renewed his proposal for marriage and again Mary accepted. They were quietly married with only close family and friends present, on November 4, 1842, and thirty-two-year-old Abraham placed on twenty-four-year-old Mary's finger, a plain gold ring engraved with "Love is eternal."[6]

The Lincoln's first home was a rented eight-by-fourteen-foot room on the second floor of the Globe Tavern. They ate their meals in the common dining room with the other tenants. For Abe, this new residence was a step up, and for Mary, a significant step down. For the first time in her life, she was without personal servants and a spacious and extravagant home. But Mary made no complaints. She was just happy to be married to Abraham and made the best of her lot. Abe was equally in love.

Abe wrote a letter to a lawyer friend and said, "Nothing new here, except my marrying, which to me, is a matter of profound wonder."[7]

On August 1, 1843, Robert Todd Lincoln was born. After his birth, Abe stopped by his dentist's office nearby to excitedly announce the miracle. He then joked that he was relieved to see his new son was whole and normal because he had feared that their child would inherit one of his long legs and one short one, like Mary's.[8] Abe and Mary adored their children.

***

In 1844, Abe felt that he was ready to set up his own law firm. He chose his young clerk, the unlikely William H. Herndon, who was nine years younger than him, as a partner.

Abe dashed up the stairs to the office where Herndon was studying and said, "Billy, do you want to enter a partnership with me in the law business?"

"Mr. Lincoln," Herndon stammered, "this is something unexpected by me—it is an undeserved honor; and yet I will gladly and thankfully accept the kind and generous offer."

Abe responded, "Billy, I can trust you if you can trust me," and for the next sixteen years "Mr. Lincoln" and "Billy" would be partners.[9]

In time, Abe found himself trying cases before the Illinois Supreme Court. By the early 1850s, the Lincoln-Herndon law firm had become the leading law firm in Springfield, taking nearly 30 percent of all of the cases in the county court.

Herndon would handle most of the tedious research while Abe spent most of his time in the courtroom representing their clients before the judges and juries. Abe, from the first day, split all fees equally with his junior partner. Abe could always be counted on to accept cases for those who could not pay. He felt that all should be entitled to the justice system.

Twice a year, Abe, along with a judge and a handful of other attorneys, would travel about the smaller towns in an eight-county area. They did this to try legal cases

where no judge or lawyers lived or practiced. With these circuit runs, Abe became acquainted with thousands of central Illinois voters, and he seemed to always remember their names and circumstances.

"All [who] claim the personal acquaintance of Mr. Lincoln," wrote one newspaperman of the day, "will agree that he is the very embodiment of good temper and affability. They will all concede that he has a kind word, an encouraging smile, a humorous remark for nearly all [who seek] his presence."[10]

One day while standing in the courthouse, directly beneath Abe's second-story law office, Edward Baker, Abe's admired friend, was making a speech and verbally attacked a local newspaper to an audience of voters.

The angered brother of the newspaper editor shouted, "Pull him down." For a moment it appeared that the crowd was about to do just that.

Abe was listening to the commotion from the floor above and sensed danger for his friend. Suddenly his long legs suddenly appeared dangling through a trapdoor that separated the two floors. He dropped onto the platform on which Baker was being threatened.

Abe tried in vain to calm the angry crowd until he seized a stone water jug and shouted, "I'll break it over the head of the first man who lays a hand on Baker." Thus silencing the audience, he continued in a perfect calmness, "Hold on, gentlemen, let us not disgrace the age and country in which we live. This is a land where freedom of speech is guaranteed. Mr. Baker has a right to speak and ought to be permitted to do so. I am here to protect him and no man shall take him from this stand if I can prevent him." Order was then restored.[11]

Chapter Five

Congressman Lincoln

In the cold winter of 1846, Mary and Abe were blessed with the birth of their second son, Edward Baker Lincoln, named after Abe's friend who he rescued from angry voters. This year also brought about Abe's next political race—his third try at the US House of Representatives. This campaign for Congress forced him to share his religious position. His opponent in this election was Peter Cartwright, a tough-talking, circuit-riding preacher. Reverend Cartwright was renowned for having baptized more that seven thousand converts into his Methodist faith.

During the campaign, Reverend Cartwright often told the people that Abe scoffed at Christians and their faith. During the campaign, Abe attended one of Reverend Cartwright's sermons. The Reverend asked all to stand who wanted to go to heaven. Many of the listeners stood up. The preacher then asked those who didn't want to go to hell to stand. All stood up—except Abe.

Cartwright looked gravely at the congregation and said, "I observe that many responded to the first invitation to give their hearts to God and to go to heaven. And

I further observe that all of you save one indicated that you did not desire to go to hell. The sole exception is Mr. Lincoln, who did not respond to either invitation. May I inquire of you, Mr. Lincoln, where you are going?"

It was not Abe's intention to interfere with Reverend Cartwright's sermon. He was disappointed that the reverend had called him out. But at his question Abe rose slowly and replied, "I came here as a respectful listener. I did not know that I was to be singled out by Brother Cartwright. I believe in treating religious matters with due solemnity. I admit that the questions propounded by Brother Cartwright are of great importance. I did not feel called upon to answer as the rest of you did. Brother Cartwright asks me directly where I am going. I desire to reply with equal directness: I am going to Congress."[1]

Cartwright was not alone in condemning Abe for his religion, or lack thereof as they supposed. While Abe often attended church, and even taught a Sunday School class, he did not become a member of any church. But he was an avid reader of the Bible and knew its contents and could recite its messages better than most preachers.

If keeping the Christian commandments serves as a measure of one's love for God, perhaps few mortals surpass Abe Lincoln in living the commandments and loving God and his fellowmen.

Cartwright's ridicule of Abe's religious beliefs had little effect in this election. The voters in the district elected him to the US House of Representatives by a large margin.

***

Not long after Abe returned from Washington, death returned to his family. Their young son Eddy died on February 1, 1850. He was not quite four years old.

The family thought that it was consumption; however, researchers today believe it was tuberculosis. Later that year, Mary Lincoln gave birth to William Wallace, who was born on December 21, 1850. The Lincolns hoped the arrival of their third son would help ease the grief caused by Edward's death, but it did not. Even ten years later, Mary's eyes would fill with tears at the very mention of Eddy's name.

Abe loved children. One day, neighborhood boys strung a string across the path to knock off Abe's tall stovepipe hat as he walked by. He retrieved the hat, rounded up the boys, and took them around the corner to buy them some cookies. He played handball with the older boys and, on his hands and knees, would teach them to play marbles. When the circus came to town, he would round up the boys and girls whose parents were too poor to pay the admission, and with his sons, they would enjoy the wonders there. Once he noticed a small boy beating time on a pan in the alley behind his house. When Christmas came around, Abe made sure that a real drum was waiting for him on Christmas morning.

Holding no public office, he settled into this next chapter of his life. He focused more attention on his sons, his wife, his home, and his career. During the next decade, the small Lincoln home would experience a number of remodels and expansions, adding an upstairs for the growing family. In 1853, their fourth son, Thomas, was born to them, named after Abe's father. Abe nicknamed him Tad because as a baby Tad had a large head and a tiny body. Abe thought he looked like a tadpole.

***

At age forty, Abe Lincoln was back riding the circuit

with the reputation for honesty and skill as a lawyer. He seemed incapable of any degree of dishonesty, and he continued to charge low fees for his services. Even late in his career, Abe wrote to a man who had sent him a check for twenty-five dollars for drawing up some legal papers, saying that the man had paid him too much. "Fifteen dollars is enough for the job,"[2] and he returned ten dollars with the letter.

For the next eleven years, Abe, now a senior lawyer on the traveling circuit, would follow Judge David Davis on the Eight Judicial District to take on as much work for his nominal fees as he could. They were quite a mismatched pair. Judge Davis was a heavy man—immaculate in his appearance and manner. Conversely, Abe was tall and thin and didn't seem to care a lick for his appearance. He wore pants that rarely reached his shoe tops, and in summer, he wore a white linen jacket that was stained and tattered.

The peaceful and prosperous years following Abe's return from Congress were laced with melancholy as he pondered the uncertainties of his future.

He once confided in Herndon, "How hard, oh how hard it is to die and leave one's Country no better than if one had never lived in it."[3]

His current course in life did little to sustain his inner and closely guarded sense that he was born to a high purpose. He longed to make his country better.

Herndon observed that some days Abe would arrive at the office in a cheerful mood, only to fall into to a quiet gloomy one. He would rest his chin in his palm and stare out the window for hours as he pondered his future.

To the great misfortune of millions, the United States Constitution possessed a serious flaw in it. The

Constitution recognized slavery as a legal practice. With all his heart, Abe had always wanted to see the slaves freed. But his reverence for the Constitution that allowed for slavery kept him from joining abolition groups to end it. Despite this, he and the new Republican Party were determined to block the spread of slavery in the new territories and future states. In this way they could at least control its evil spread and do so within the law.

Slavery was the prominent political, moral, and social issue of the day. But during these years Abe remained apart from all political activities. It was Abe's longtime political nemesis, Stephen A. Douglas—arguably the most prominent politician in America—that brought Abe roaring back into the national political arena. While Abe's modest political career appeared to have ended, his frequent rival was at the top of his political game. Stephen A. Douglas had become this nation's most powerful US senator and a candidate for president in 1852.

Abe's abrupt return to politics in 1854 would change his life profoundly and start him on the pathway from being relatively unknown to becoming the greatest of American presidents. In that year, Congress had passed, and President Franklin Pierce had signed into law, Stephen A. Douglas's Kansas-Nebraska Act and the accompanying repeal of the Missouri Compromise.

This new law caused Abe to say that Stephen A. Douglas, "Took us by surprise—astounded us. . . . We were thunderstruck and stunned."[4]

What was it about the passing of this act, five years after his political retirement, that roused him so? Abe believed this law created a danger to the nation's very existence. The act allowed Kansas and Nebraska, and all territories and states that would follow, to choose to have or not have slavery in their territories.

Abe would soon publicly declare that the Kansas-Nebraska Act removed the moral injustice of slavery and turned it into something that was not wrong. It now would be socially acceptable. This law would make the nation morally neutral regarding slavery, and "he saw this moral neutrality as [a] grave threat to the future survival of this nation and its culture of freedoms."[5]

The door was now open for citizens of the future states west of the Mississippi River to *choose* to legalize slavery in their respective territories and states. With the passage of the Kansas-Nebraska Act, slavery had essentially become legitimized. The act removed slavery from the moral wrong it had always been to a quality-of-life option for white Americans.

Abe was deeply troubled at what he saw. This government, which he believed to be created under God by the Founding Fathers, was now placed on a dangerous path toward its own self-destruction. While many future states would probably choose against slavery, Stephen A. Douglas and the contentious political leaders of the South were certain that many other states would vote for slavery.

And with his long-held conviction that this nation could not survive, "half slave and half free,"[6] and that a "house divided against itself"[7] could not long endure, Abe was stirred to the depths of his soul. Racism and white supremacy would now be legal and celebrated in America with the passage of the Kansas-Nebraska Act. And the ingenious Abe Lincoln had made a decision that he would somehow stop it.

Chapter Six

What Was He Thinking?

After Congress passed this bill, Abe could no longer stay out of the political arena as he had for the past five years. The Kansas-Nebraska Act introduced dangers that he could not allow.

So naturally he started to study. He researched speeches, newspapers, the *Congressional Globe,* and history. The local newspaper reported that Abe was "mousing about the libraries in the State House" and "nosing for weeks in the State Library, pumping his brain and his imagination for points and arguments" or anything related to events that had led to this moral collapse.[1] He read Douglas's senate speeches defending the bill on the one side and the speeches of those who opposed it on the other.

What Abe nor anyone else could know, was that he, a mere retired politician and prairie lawyer, with a less than notable national political career, was only six years from the White House. And he was mounting the most remarkable and unlikely political assent in United States history.

As a backlash to Douglas's Kansas-Nebraska Act, the

Democratic support in the Senate from Iowa and Maine collapsed. Some of Senator Stephen Douglas's supporters disapproved of the Kansas-Nebraska Act too. In an attempt to rally more support, Douglas returned to Illinois in his luxurious personal train car. This special train car had a small cannon mounted on the top, and a brass band to announce his arrival.

With passion and eloquence, Douglas spoke to the people of Illinois and explained that the Kansas-Nebraska Act merely granted citizens the right to choose if their state would allow slavery or not. However, to halt Douglas's progress, the "aroused, thunderstruck, and well-prepared Abraham Lincoln"[2] launched a dramatic single-handed assault on this new corruption that the United States Congress and President Pierce had passed.

Abe began his astounding national emergence when Douglas arrived in Bloomington, Illinois, to speak to a Democratic gathering on September 29, 1854. Abe traveled to Bloomington to hear Senator Douglas's speech. Here, he proposed to Douglas that they hold a debate on the dreadful law just passed. But Douglas refused to debate him. Douglas had just won the contest at the highest level in Congress, and the president had signed his bill into law. Douglas had already won.

Plus he knew Abe, and he knew Abe was a strong debater from their numerous encounters in earlier years on opposite sides of the Illinois legislature. Douglas had nothing to gain by debating his victory with a lightweight prairie lawyer. His aim was to recapture the support of his now troubled local voters by presenting just his side of the argument and nothing else.

Abe had astounding moral courage in challenging

Douglas and the national government. He was nowhere in terms of prominence on the national political scene. What made him think that his challenge to the most powerful politician in America would be taken seriously?

Douglas was no easy opponent for experienced politicians, let alone for beginners. "He was a practiced, powerful debater, full of energy, articulate, sarcastic, scathing, and formidable."[3] He left some of the nation's most distinguished political figures "gasping, vanquished, and silenced" in his wake.[4]

Abe knew his chances for success were small, but he knew he was right. What could a common citizen, mostly unknown outside of his home state, do to change a bill that had been passed in Congress and signed into law by the president? Yet that is exactly what Abe would accomplish. Unlike many men Abe had no personal agendas or ambitions to fulfill. Instead, his debates became proclamations to the nation of the basic principles of right and wrong, especially the moral wrongs of slavery.

Six years later and days before his presidential election, he confided in a friend, "I know there is a God and that He hates injustice and slavery. I see the storm coming and I know that His hand is in it. *If he has a place and a work for me, and I think he has, I believe I am ready.* I am nothing, but truth is everything. I know I am right because I know that liberty is right, for Christ teaches it and Christ is God."[5]

At the conclusion of the Civil War to a group of freed slaves in Richmond who were bowing to him and addressing him as their savior, he said, "You must kneel to God only and thank Him for the liberty you now enjoy. I am but God's humble instrument."[6]

From 1854 onward, this "peculiarsome" boy, so kind, obedient, and thirsty for knowledge, this "lawyer who was never known to lie,"[7] was about to become the unsponsored conscience for the nation. And to what aim? Abe strictly focused on healing the nation from slavery.

After Douglas's refusal to debate, Abe listened quietly to Douglas's defiant and snarling message in Bloomington. When Douglas finished his rant, some in the crowd unexpectedly called for Abe to give a response. Honoring Douglas's earlier refusal to debate, he declined. But he did announce that he would speak later that evening in a separate meeting if anyone wanted to listen.

Many came to listen, and he gave the first of what would become a long series of messages challenging the immorality of slavery. Abe's daring challenge was written in many major newspapers. Over the next six years, this press coverage helped catapult Abe into the presidency by making his name known throughout the nation.

This rebuttal speech marked the beginning of a new Abe. Even though he wasn't the only antislavery voice in the North, his fresh voice and perspective resonated with people. He focused on the principles of immorality found in slavery and the importance of unity in the nation. He didn't include personal attacks in his speeches like so many politicians did. He didn't accuse, judge, or criticize an opponent's character or their self-promoting themes. He focused on principles and on doing one's duty to God and his country.

Abe said, "I must trust in that Supreme Being who has never forsaken this favored land."[8]

He often said that the people had an obligation not just to this nation but also to the rest of the world to protect and defend the liberties given to them by their Constitution. He repeatedly reminded his listeners of their responsibility to remember and honor God, the Founding Fathers, the Declaration of Independence, and the Constitution. Abe's voice was a new voice, a prophet-like voice in America. He had the ability to speak from a spiritual plane that was free from hypocrisy, dishonesty, and pride. His messages were directed to the "better angels"[9] of the souls in Americans. Yes, he was God's chosen instrument, God's everyday hero sent to change America and his lasting influence changed the world.

In his speech to the large Bloomington crowd, Abe erupted with deep emotion to join the fight against slavery and against the Southern states' increasing threats to leave the Union.

He said, "It's wrong; it's wrong in its effect, letting slavery into Kansas and Nebraska—and wrong in principle, allowing it to spread to every other part of the wide world, where men can be found inclined to take it. When we were political slaves of King George, and wanted to be free, we called the maxim that 'all men are created equal' a self-evident truth; but now . . . we have grown fat, and have lost the dread of being slaves ourselves."[10]

Abe knew that the Kansas-Nebraska Act introduced enslaving "one man by another" as morally right, and he knew that was a lie.[11]

Senator Douglas viewed slavery as a political nuisance, an obstacle to his other political goals. But he frequently spoke of black people with sneering disdain.

Abe believed the people of Nebraska to be good people, but "no man is good enough to govern another man, without that other's consent."[12]

Abe's passion increased along with Douglas's frustration. Douglas had no desire to allow Abe's inspiring words to be heard alongside his. On October 3, Douglas was the keynote speaker for the Illinois state fair in Abe's hometown of Springfield. Rain was expected for that day so the speech was moved to the State House. Again Abe was present but instead of sitting in the audience, he paced back and forth in the lobby as he listened intently to Douglas's fiery speech. After Douglas concluded his speech, Abe suddenly appeared on the stairway and shouted to the dispersing crowd that he would answer Douglas on the morrow. Out of fairness, he invited Douglas to be present and offered him time following his remarks for a rebuttal.

Douglas had no choice but to accept. This gallant stairway challenge would mark the rise of Abe Lincoln in America. The next day the hall was full to capacity as Abe took the podium. He reached the heart of his disagreement by asserting that slavery depended upon "whether a Negro is *not* or *is* a man."[13]

He said, "[Douglas] has no very vivid impression that the Negro is a human; and consequently has no idea that there can be any moral question in legislating about him."[14]

But Abe argued that a black was very much a man. He reminded them that the Declaration of Independence teaches that all men are created equal. Because a black is a man, there could be no moral right to enslave him. The institution of slavery was founded in the selfishness of man's nature.

The audience was moved by Abe's moral outrage as he described "the monstrous injustice of slavery."[15]

"There can be no moral right in connection with one

man's making a slave of another,"[16] he thundered. "Our revolutionary fathers"[17] knew that slavery was wrong, but they could not end it at the time they organized the new government. The Founding Fathers refused to put the word "slavery" in the Constitution. They only allowed references to it.

Abe could not hide his indignation at Douglas's claim that he and the proslavery movement were merely acting in the spirit of the Founding Fathers.

Abe opened his audience's vision to the magnitude of damage that American slavery would mean to this nation and the rest of the world. The world's best hope depended on the continuation of a strong and free union of states, united in purpose.

"We are proclaiming ourselves political hypocrites before the world by thus fostering Human Slavery and proclaiming ourselves, at the same time, the sole friends of Human Freedom,"[18] Abe said.

It was another remarkable and moving speech. Women in the audience waved their white handkerchiefs and the men gave loud and continuous hurrahs. With these three speeches in the fall of 1854, Abe launched himself from a has-been politician to a formidable contender for the "Little Giant," Stephen A. Douglas—the most feared and powerful politician in America.

Chapter Seven

The Unlikely President

As 1860 approached, newspapers throughout the country began revealing potential candidates for the upcoming presidential election. A handful mentioned Abe Lincoln. No one seemed to take the suggestions very seriously. Of all the names suggested, Abe was clearly the least qualified of the group.

He knew the odds were stacked against him. At the age of fifty, he was old. People didn't live long in those days. He didn't come from lots of money or even have formal schooling. Sure, he loved to study the writings of the Founding Fathers, but he had very little experience with government. As for holding an actual office he had some experience in the House of Representatives, but for the previous ten years he had been absent in the political world. There was one other force that kept his eye on the office of presidency of the United States—his wife, Mary. She believed that her husband had all the right tools to make a great president. She encouraged him continually to pursue the office.

Another thing that he had in his favor was the highly popular debates with Stephen A. Douglas in 1858. The entire nation followed his masterful challenge to the strongest politician in America. Here he proved himself to be a contender for the presidency.

The Democratic Party, which promoted the expansion of slavery and open immigration to the United States, remained the dominant political party. The remaining smaller parties possessed far too few votes to advance their agendas. Three of these weaker parties wisely joined forces to form the new Republican Party. The primary political position of this new Republican Party would be to bring an end to slavery.

Their candidate would compete against the leading Democratic Party candidate, Stephen A. Douglas, along with lesser candidates John Bell and John C. Breckinridge. Running for the Republican ticket against other notable and successful politicians, such as William H. Seward, former governor of New York; Salmon P. Chase, former governor of Ohio, was a difficult challenge for Abe.

Like today, anyone could run for president in the mid 1800s. Like today, the primary elections take place to select one candidate for each political party. In 1860, four candidates ran for the Republican Party. Abe recognized his weak position against these better-qualified rivals, but he was unafraid to challenge them. To create a wider circulation of his ideas, he quietly compiled and published his debates with Stephen A. Douglas. The 268-page book became an immediate bestseller. In December 1859, he published his autobiography.

This unlikely candidate from Illinois fascinated people in the East. Abe received an invitation by New York voters to lecture in Manhattan with two other notable presidential candidates. Many expected "something weird, rough and uncultivated"[1] from him. And at first glance they were not disappointed.

George Haven Putnam was in the audience and wrote, "The long ungainly figure, upon which hung clothes that, while new for the trip, were evidently the work of an unskilled tailor; the large feet; the clumsy hands, of which . . . the orator seemed to be unduly conscious; the long gaunt head capped by a shock of hair that seemed not to have been thoroughly brushed out made a picture which did not fit in with New York's conception of a finished statesman."[2]

But the speech that Abe delivered erased any evidence of a backward frontiersman. He attacked Douglas's assertion that the Founding Fathers wanted slavery in America to remain. He demonstrated that slavery was a violation of the sacred Declaration of Independence's position that all men are created equal, what these great men fought for. Abe portrayed all Republicans as a party with a mission to preserve the legacy of the Founding Fathers against the assault of the proslavery movement.

"Let us have faith," he admonished, "that right makes might, and in that faith, let us, to the end, dare to do our duty as we understand it."[3]

His delivery was frequently interrupted by enthusiastic applause. When he closed, the crowd was so excited by his speech that they jumped to their feet and applauded, waving their hats and handkerchiefs.

Noah Brooks of the *New York Tribune* wrote, "He's the greatest man since St. Paul."

A Harvard student told his father, "It was the best speech I ever heard."[4]

The following day, four New York papers printed the entire speech. It was immediately published in pamphlet form and issued as a Republican tract in newspapers from New York, Chicago, Albany, and Detroit. In all, it was a superb political development for the unlikely candidate. During his two weeks in New England, he would speak nearly every day.

In those days, candidates didn't openly campaign for office. This required other people to push candidates forward and promote them to voters. After a night of reflection, Abe consented to allow a number of friends to quietly work toward it.

These friends felt that Abe's integrity was a potential weakness in the aggressive campaign arena. One of the campaign managers, Judge David Davis explained, "Lincoln has few of the qualities of a politician and cannot do much personally to advance his interests, because he was such, 'a guileless man.' "[5]

While his managers were set to the task, Abe remained on the sidelines. He deflected requests for political statements by saying, "When not a very great man begins to be mentioned for a very great position, his head is likely to be a little turned."[6]

***

One week prior to the National Republican Convention in Chicago, the Illinois State Republican Convention was held in Decatur. Lacking a campaign slogan like President Harrison's "Log Cabin and Hard Cider" and Andrew Jackson's "Old Hickory," one of Abe's supporters came up with one for Abe as the Illinois Republican nomination for president. Consulting with the aged John Hanks, a cousin to Abe's mother Lucy, they located a split rail fence near Decatur that Hanks and Abe had built thirty years before. On the first day of the convention, the elderly Hanks marched down the aisle followed by two of the old fence rails decorated with flags and streamers. On the fence rails someone had written,

ABRAHAM LINCOLN
THE RAIL CANDIDATE
FOR PRESIDENT IN 1860
TWO RAILS FROM A LOT OF 3,000 MADE IN 1830 BY THOS. HANKS AND ABE LINCOLN—WHOSE FATHER WAS THE FIRST PIONEER OF MACON COUNTY

The crowd erupted into a deafening cheer and applause for Abe, who was called to the stand. While blushing, he confirmed that he had indeed built a cabin and split the log rails that surrounded it thirty years ago. The cheers that followed his remarks suggested that even his friends had underestimated his popularity. He would now be labeled "The Rail Splitter," a self-made man.

Beginning with George Washington, all American presidents were either military heroes or well-known politicians. But Abe would prove that even a poor frontier woodcutter and rail splitter can become the leader of this great nation.

The next day, Abe was unanimously selected as the Illinois Republican choice for president of the United States for Chicago's National convention the following week.

In those days the candidates did not attend the national political conventions either. Abe truly wanted to be there but told a friend that, "he was almost too much of a candidate to go, and not quite enough to stay home."[7]

He stayed home. The pressure to not openly seek the office did not prevent the nonstop political wrangling, positioning, promises, and bribes from occurring as each candidate's managers labored for the nomination. There were whisperings of unethical dealings, but Abe's men knew that he would have no part of them. In fact, one friend sent a telegram to Abe, encouraging him to consider a deal with others who promised him their votes. But Abe flatly refused their offer. He would not go against his principles of right and wrong, even if it cost him the presidency.

On the day when the delegates cast their votes, Abe passed part of the nervous day playing "fives," a form of handball with some men in the vacant lot next to the *Illinois State Journal*, which housed the telegraph machine and operator. As was the usual procedure, the delegates in Chicago would cast their votes in rounds and the first candidate to garner 233 votes would win the nomination.

As expected, the first round went to the Republican Party favorite William Seward, who received 173 votes. But to the surprise of all, Abe received 102 votes, with the others trailing far behind.

In the second round, Seward's votes increased to 184; Abe's also increased to 181. All the other candidates fell further behind. In the third round, Seward received nearly the same number, whereas the majority of the remaining delegates flocked to Abe's corner; and the final tally gave Abe 364 votes out of a possible 466. Seward's delegates then followed suit and backed Abe as well.

Remarkably, Abe Lincoln was the unanimous choice for the Republican candidate for president of the United

States. The nomination was won with no hidden promises or deals. He won the election not as a strong campaigner—he did not campaign. He won on the platform of integrity.

When Abe received news of his victory, he approached his ballplayer friends and joked, "Gentlemen, you had better come up and shake my hand while you can—honors elevate some men."[8] Then he headed for home, telling them, "There is a little woman at our house who is probably more interested in this dispatch than I am."[9]

Abe's integrity played a key role in his victory. Many people didn't agree with his political views, but he won their respect because of the respect he showed them, including his opponents. He said nothing offensive to his opponents, which made it difficult for them to speak poorly of him. Abe's character served him well once again.

***

The citizens of Springfield were beside themselves to think that one of their own was a candidate for president. They flocked to the Lincoln home on Eighth and Jackson streets to express their support. Outside of Springfield, the northern half of the nation wanted to know about this unexpected candidate. Abe was flooded with telegrams, letters, photographers, and reporters. Nearly 200,000 additional autobiographical sketches were printed and distributed. Despite his popularity in the North, few in the South had interest in him.

Abe would now run against three other presidential candidates, fellow Illinoisan Stephen A. Douglas and former Vice President John C. Breckinridge from Kentucky. The fourth candidate was John Bell. Again, Abe remained on the sidelines, pledging to make no political speeches during the campaign. He only said that if elected he would procure "Justice and fairness to all."[10]

Abe's major opponent, Stephen A. Douglas, ignored tradition and traveled the country to promote himself in the race. Abe remained in Springfield, while huge rallies were taking place throughout the North in his absence conducted by his campaign committee and fellow Republicans. Oddly, his silence worked to his advantage because it gave his opponents little to criticize.

State elections took place one month prior to the November 6 presidential election. Everyone anxiously awaited those results. The Republicans conducted a brilliant campaign resulting in several historically Democratic states voting for Republican candidates. This was good news for Abe in November.

On Election Day, Abe was reluctant to vote, not wanting to appear to vote for himself. Nonetheless, sensing the importance of the voting process he walked to the voting station amid cheers from the local citizens. He cut off the top portion of the ballot that contained his name and the others for president, then cast his votes for his choice in the other races. That evening he joined the Republicans in the state capitol to hear the voting results as they arrived by telegraph.

After years of success and influence in Illinois, Stephen A. Douglas also watched with his Democratic supporters, as his home state of Illinois went Republican and backed Abe. Indiana and a number of other Western states followed suit. But the critical returns would be those from the Eastern States.

By ten o'clock that evening, word arrived that Pennsylvania had surprisingly voted Republican. At two o'clock in the morning, word finally arrived that the important state of New York also went Republican, sealing the election for Abe. Abe Lincoln, the Rail Splitter and Self-Made Man. He would be the next president of the United States, and he won it without a single vote from ten of the Southern states.

Abe recalled, "I went home, but not to get much sleep for I then felt as I never had before, the responsibility that was upon me."[11]

The stressful race was finally over. This everyday hero was now president of the United States. But Abe's election didn't come without heavy opposition from the South. The day after his victory, people in Florida hung a human figure made of straw by the neck, saying this was Abe.

The *Dallas Herald* wrote, "Evil days are upon us."[12] The *Augusta Constitutional* declared, "The South should arm at once."[13] Within days of Abe's election, seven states in the South seceded from the United States and formed a new country. They called themselves the Confederate States of America. Four more southern states followed their dramatic separation from the United States.

South Carolina became the first of the total eleven states to withdraw from the Union.

Representatives were promptly dispatched to all parts of the South to carry the message that South Carolina had declared its independence and invited her Southern sister states to join her.

Chapter Eight

Off to Washington

Abe didn't make any public statements or formal addresses in the four months between his November election to his inauguration in March. Instead, he quietly observed the unraveling of this nation while President James Buchanan finished out his term.

Politicians in Washington could not agree on how to respond to the startling secession of the Southern states. Some called for a Constitutional amendment to offer even more favors for the Southern slave owners. The House of Representatives recommended a Constitutional amendment that would prohibit any further interference with slavery in hopes of calming the Southern agitators. The Senate offered up additional concessions to pacify their rebellious neighbors.

But Abe, observing all of this in Springfield, was determined that he would not bargain with the Southern rebels.

In early February 1861, just days before the Lincoln family's second move to Washington, Abe made one last visit to his beloved stepmother, now seventy-three and widowed in Coles County. He went to the small, two-room cabin that he had helped his father build. His stepmother, Sarah Bush Lincoln, shared the home with her daughter. He gave her a black woolen dress and paid his respects to his deceased father by carving his initials, T. L., into two stakes and placing them at the head and foot of his grave.

He then bade her farewell, fearing that this would be his final good-bye to the loving woman who restored motherly warmth to his young and grieving boyhood.

Sarah recalled later, "I did not want him elected—was afraid somehow or other . . . that something would happen to him . . . and that I should see him no more."[1]

Her loving stepson tried to comfort her by saying, "No no mama, trust in the Lord and all will be well. We will see each other again."[2] Sadly, his mother's premonition would prove to be accurate.

On a cold and rainy February 11, 1861, the Presidential Special, a train consisting of only two cars painted a bright yellow, hissed and steamed. It waited for the president-elect's arrival at the Springfield train station. The train was ready to carry Abe to Washington and to the most severe crisis to ever face any United States president.

Abe had requested that his departure be done quietly and without fanfare. But around one thousand friends and well-wishers surrounded the train station and waited in the rain for Springfield's favorite son to arrive.

That morning, Abe made one last visit to his law office with his law partner, William Herndon. "Billy," he said, "over sixteen years together, and we have not had a cross word during all that time, have we?"

"No, indeed we have not," Billy replied.

"Don't take the sign down, Billy; let it swing, that our clients may understand that the election of a president makes no change in the firm of Lincoln & Herndon. If I live, I'm coming back, and we will go right on practicing law as if nothing had ever happened."[3] Then the two went down the stairs and across the town to the railroad station. Abe never returned alive.

Herndon recorded, "The sorrow of parting from his old associations was deeper than most persons would imagine."[4] Abe had begun experiencing a "feeling which had become irrepressible that he would never return alive."[5]

Abe stepped out on the platform among a chorus of cheers and calls for a speech. He hadn't planned on giving a speech that day nor at any of the dozens of stops along the way, except for a select few preplanned locations.

A reporter near the new president observed, "Lincoln's face was pale, and quivered with emotion so deep as to render him almost unable to utter a single word."[6]

Moved with emotion at the fond support of so many friends, he removed his beaver hat and motioned for silence.

The nation had heard nothing from their new leader for the four months since his election. In the face of the recent alarming events of secession, they were desperate to hear from this stranger into whose hands they had placed the survival of the nation. The reporters eagerly readied their pencils at this unexpected opportunity to record his unplanned remarks.

Struggling to gather himself, and with the warmest sincerity, he said, "My friends, no one, not in my situation, can appreciate my feelings of sadness at this parting.

To this place, and the kindness of these people, I owe everything. Here I have been a quarter of a century, and have passed from a young to an old man. Here my children have been born, and one is buried. I now leave, not knowing when, or whether ever, I may return, with a task before me greater than that which rested upon Washington.

"Without the assistance of that Divine Being, who ever attended him, I cannot succeed. With that assistance I cannot fail. . . . Let us confidently hope that all will yet be well. . . . I bid you an affectionate farewell."[7]

James C. Conkling, a close friend to Abe recorded that "many eyes were filled to overflowing." And Abe's "breast heaved with emotion and he could scarcely command his feelings sufficiently to commence."[8]

In the twelve days and nights that his train rumbled across the states from Springfield to Washington, Americans saw Abe more than any other president before him. He gave nearly one hundred speeches during the twelve-day journey. It became too difficult to be unresponsive to the cheering and anxious crowds.

He was hesitant to make unplanned speeches. He knew how easily a misspoken or misinterpreted phrase could ignite more instability in the nation that was teetering at the edge of a cliff. He was also keenly aware that President Buchanan continued as president until Abe's March 4 Inauguration. But the national and local newspapers were gobbling up every word he spoke for their anxious readers back home. Millions in America read details of the journey and of his speeches. His enemies in the South were as hungry to read them as anyone, as they looked for clues signaling his course of action as president.

Abe used these speeches to reveal to Americans the principles he would use to lead this country. He viewed himself as an instrument in God's hands. God's will would be sought and then followed. He assured them that God would see them through this national crisis.

In New Jersey, he declared, "I shall be most happy indeed if I shall be an humble instrument in the hands of the Almighty, and of this his almost chosen people."[9]

In Trenton, he revealed his belief that his role as president came "not only from the people but from *the Almighty*,"[10] and that the present crisis was about nothing less than the *salvation* of the nation. Abe also calmed America with his wit and wisdom. There were frequent reports of cheering laughter from the crowds.

Abe believed that the liberties of this free nation, which were won and organized by the Founding Fathers, had been severely eroded and weakened. He saw it as his role and that of all other political leaders to defend those hard-won liberties.

Abe's Presidential Special wasn't the only train being closely watched by the nation. On February 11, the newly elected president of the Confederacy, Jefferson Davis, was also zigzagging through the South by train from his plantation in Mississippi to the new Confederate Capital in Montgomery, Alabama.

Chapter Nine

I, Abraham Lincoln, Do Solemnly Swear

Never before had a presidential inauguration taken place in such a tense and dangerous atmosphere. Riflemen lined the rooftops and cannons were set near the capital to nervously guard the life of the new United States president. Abe made his way toward the Capitol in a cavalry-flanked horse-drawn carriage accompanied by the worn out President James Buchanan. Many of the Washington residents were overwhelmingly sympathetic to the South and opposed Abe. Wild rumors swirled, fed by many of the Southerners who felt trapped in Washington. They speculated about attacks on Washington or assassination attempts on the president-elect.

The citizens of Washington City had tolerated the Democrat James Buchanan, but this Abe, a Republican, was viewed as an unwelcome intrusion.

At noon on March 4, the carriage of President James Buchanan and President-elect Abe Lincoln proceeded down Pennsylvania Avenue. There appeared to be as many soldiers and sharpshooters as citizens. Few of the anti-Lincoln locals attended the event, but some twenty-five thousand, mostly from the nearby Northern states, were present on that cold and gray day.

Abe rose to address the audience, fully aware of their anxiety. He was momentarily distracted with no place to put his tall stovepipe hat when Stephen A. Douglas, sitting behind him stepped forward saying, "Permit me sir,"[1] and held his hat during the ceremony.

With his inaugural address, Abe expressed that he believed that states didn't have a Constitutional right to secede from the Union. As the president of the United States, he would defend the Union. And though he despised slavery, he had no intention of interfering with it in the states where it was lawfully practiced. He didn't want the people from the South to be his enemy. He considered them to be his friends and fellow citizens.

"In *your* hands, my dissatisfied fellow countrymen, and not *mine* is the momentous issue of civil war," Abe said to the Southern agitators. "*You* have no oath registered in Heaven to destroy the government, while I shall have the most solemn one to 'preserve, protect and defend it.' "[2]

With warmth and sincerity, Abe conclude his speech, "I am loath to close. We are not enemies, but friends. We must not be enemies. The mystic chords of memory . . . will yet swell the chorus of the Union, when again touched, as surely they will be, by the better angels of our nature."[3]

At the end of the speech, the eighty-four-year-old Chief Justice Roger Taney stepped forward to swear in the new president. With his left hand on an open Bible, and right hand raised to a square, Abe repeated the oath of office, "I, Abraham Lincoln, do solemnly swear that I will faithfully execute the office of President of the United States, and will, to the best of my ability, preserve, protect, and defend the Constitution of the United States."[4]

To the astonishment of the Southern agitators, he would keep this solemn promise.

While his cabinet and Congress did not know how to respond to the Southern rebellion, Abe had a plan. The people of the North grew impatient waiting, but the Confederacy's open aggression at Fort Sumter brought everything into focus. Abe intended to keep Fort Sumter. This strategically located fortress in the Charleston, South Carolina, harbor was surrounded by a company of Confederate soldiers with over one hundred cannons awaiting orders to fire upon it. Abe had thought long about how to address this crisis. He calculated that if the South Carolinians made the fatal mistake of attacking Fort Sumter that it would electrify the Northern citizens to action.

He was right. On April 12, the Confederacy fired upon and took Fort Sumter. The day after the attack, Abe issued a proclamation. To the horror of the Southern citizens, he called for 75,000 volunteers to join the Union army and suppress the Southern rebellion. With enthusiasm, the North rallied behind their new president.

Abe's Northern supporters were confident that they were stronger than the South. There were twenty million people in the North compared to the South's nine million, not to mention the North's far superior resources. The *Chicago Tribune* predicted success "within two to three months at the furthest," because, "Illinois can whip the South by herself."[5]

Abe did not share the same feelings. He reminded them that the Northerners and Southerners have similar characteristics and abilities. He expected a long conflict ahead. Again he was right.

Abe nervously went to church on Sunday morning, July 21, as the Battle of Bull Run began. At six o'clock, news arrived at the White House that the Union Army was in full retreat. The Confederate Army had prevailed. That was not how it was supposed to be! By nightfall on that summer Sunday, more than 4,800 men from both sides lay dead on the battlefield.

Abe knew all to well the depth of anguish that the loss of a loved one can bring. Death had already taken his infant brother, his dearly loved mother, his only sister and sibling, his sweetheart Ann Rutledge, then his son Eddie. Abe and Mary were just months away from the death of their cherished son Willie. He felt overwhelmed with grief knowing the key part he now played in the death of these thousands of men and boys. For a man such as Abe, who could not pass a small pig mired in the mud without easing its suffering, the next four years of unrelenting casualty reports would bring him untold sorrow. He would anguish with the rest of the nation through the long crisis.

Along with the tragic losses of soldiers, Abe felt the future unity of the country slipping away from him. While the North was mired in setbacks, the South was jubilant with their success.

In late 1861, the tide turned. The Union enjoyed a run of victories at Port Royal, Fort Henry, and Fort Donelson thanks to little-known General Ulysses S. Grant. But with the victories came the death counts of tens of thousands of soldiers. In April 1862, General Grant won again at Shiloh, the bloodiest battle of the war thus far, but the victory left the North stunned with its thirteen thousand Union casualties.

The nation realized that it would take time to build

the kind of army that could defeat the growing Southern forces. For the next few months, Abe had a small break from the intense political pressures and the chaos of war. During these months he focused on his family and their new huge home. The thirty-one rooms in the executive mansion completely overwhelmed the Lincolns. Then they learned that not all the rooms belonged to them.

Except for the dining room, the first floor was open to all visitors. Anybody who wanted could stroll in and out of the Lincoln's home at any hour of the day and on into the evening. And stroll in they did! The White House was nearly always full of visitors, office seekers, and church groups on missions to pray with the new president and correct his misguided vision and handling of the crisis at hand. On the second floor almost half of the rooms were also public, so that the private quarters of the Lincolns' "mansion," turned out to be surprisingly small.

Abe's sons Willie and Tad enjoyed their time with the soldiers of the Bucktail Pennsylvania regiment. They conducted their own military maneuvers with the neighborhood boys they had recruited. The boys commandeered the White House rooftop for their fort, complete with painted logs for cannons, which they earnestly fired at imagined Confederates across the river.

Once a great commotion was heard from the upstairs oval room. People rushed in and found the president of the United States on his back in a playful wrestle with, Tad, Willie, and their friends. Often he was seen walking with his boys to the woods to enjoy time together. Abe cherished such times because they were rare while in the White House. He was said to have worked harder than any other president, continually engaged in the mountain

of work before him, from sunup to late at night.

The presence of children in the White House was rare, so people spoiled the Lincoln boys with gifts. A pony for Willie was especially loved as were the two goats that were occasionally seen occupying hallways and rooms in the White House. On one occasion, Tad harnessed one of the goats to a chair, which he used as a sled, and drove the goat into the East Room where a reception was being held. The women held up their hoop skirts as Tad hollered, circled the room with his goat, and exited out the door.

Ward Hill Lamon came to Washington with Abe to serve as marshal of the District of Columbia. He was Abe's trusted friend and former law partner in Illinois. His primary responsibly was to keep Abe alive during his Presidency. The poor man fretted every day for Abe's safety because Abe insisted that the doors of the White House always remain open to the public. Abe always made time to greet and assist visitors, no matter their rank or station in society. Here he heard their complaints and their petitions for his help. And with remarkable patience he listened to their often shortsighted solutions to the critical matters of his office.

Despite Abe's efforts, he couldn't escape the hissing of criticism. The lack of victory in the war disheartened people, and they blamed the president. Two years was too long to be in any kind of war.

Francis B. Carpenter, the artist who lived in the White House for part of 1864, "declared he 'had the saddest face I ever attempted to paint.' "[6] The alarming death counts and lack of progress in the war brought unrelenting sorrow to Abe's presidential years.

Abe's grief intensified when his young sons Willie and

Thomas became gravely ill. The bad water in the White House made them sick. Eleven-year-old Willie died from the illness, and poor Thomas suffered for several more days until he recovered. Mary was so pained by the death of Willie that she couldn't even attend his funeral service. Abe had to press on, but for several weeks he shut himself up in his room on Thursdays, the day Willie died, to grieve.

A few months later, after more crippling Union defeats, a caucus of angry senators was held. Abe discovered the unscheduled political committee meeting and confided in a friend. "What do these men want?" Abe asked, but he knew the answer. "They wish to get rid of me, and I am sometimes half disposed to gratify them. We are on the brink of destruction, and it appears to me that the Almighty is against us, and I can hardly see a ray of hope."[7]

By early 1863, many in Abe's own party wanted him removed from office. The constant pressures and disappointments from all sides left Abe exhausted.

It was under this cloud of failure and criticism that he had his own presidential rebirth that would change his presidency, the course of the war, and the course of this nation. He had labored to listen and respond to the advice and demands of his **cabinet** and from Congress with the hope of forming a unified relationship that would lead to victory. This plan hadn't worked.

After two years of trying to execute the presidency as had been expected of him, Abe came to the conclusion that the only advisor that could lead him and this nation out of this dark abyss was

Cabinet: The cabinet is a collection of advisors from different government departments like the Secretary of State, Secretary of War, and also the vice president.

the Almighty God Himself. Abe now found the determination to do what he had always wanted to do as president—make God's will his focus in the execution of his office. From this point he led the nation with God as his closest advisor.

His secretary John Hay, observed during this transformation, "I have rarely seen him more serene and busy. He is managing this war, the draft, foreign relations, and planning a reconstruction of the Union, all at once."[8]

Abe stunned his cabinet by revealing a vow that he made to God. If the Union Army could drive out the Confederates from Maryland, which they did just days earlier, he would interpret that as an answer from God. He would have God's approval to free the slaves in the rebelling states by issuing the Emancipation Proclamation.

"God had decided this question in favor of the slaves,"[9] he told his cabinet.

Unfortunately, our US Constitution allowed for slavery to continue in this country, and Abe would never go against the Constitution. But in the time of war, this same Constitution gave the president "war powers"—the authority to make certain additional decisions to protect the nation. With this authority, he wrote the Emancipation Proclamation, which freed the slaves only in the rebelling states. But his intent was to eventually free all the slaves.

Three months later in December of that year, Abe gave the traditional annual message to Congress in which he reinforced his decision to issue the Emancipation Proclamation. He said, "In giving freedom to the slave, we assure freedom to the free—honorable alike in what we give, and what we preserve. We shall nobly save, or meanly lose, the last best hope of earth."[10]

Many, including some of his closest friends, begged Abe to change or repeal his Emancipation Proclamation for the sake of the Union, but he "was as immovable as stone."[11] He responded to a friend that "I am a slow walker, but I never walk backwards."[12]

Abe and his Secretary of War, Edwin Stanton, proposed the next step by arming black soldiers for the Union army. Many whites believed that the experiment would be an utter failure. They were convinced that the former slaves would be poor and cowardly soldiers.

Union commanders operating throughout the South began accepting blacks that had come to them from the plantations and formed all-Negro fighting units. Within eight months, 180,000 blacks had joined ranks with the Union military forces. Most of them were emancipated slaves.

It was the Massachusetts Fifty-fourth "Colored" Infantry, under the command of a young white colonel named Robert Gould Shaw, who proved blacks would fight as hard and courageously as any white regiment when they led the assault on Fort Wagner near the Charleston harbor.

Chapter Ten

A New Birth of Freedom

In the fall of 1863, citizens needed a new dose of courage. Abe needed another message—one that would explain what the North was fighting for.

In November 1863, Abe accepted an invitation to speak at the dedication of the new National Soldier's Cemetery on the Gettysburg battlefield. He would follow the popular speaker Edward Everett to share a few words and dedicate the ground where so many lives had been lost.

Gettysburg was a bloody memory. The Union sustained a staggering 23,049 casualties in that epic Gettysburg battle. The Confederacy lost even more with 28,063 deaths.

Edward Everett arrived at the Gettysburg speakers' podium thirty minutes late, keeping the president and the crowd, estimated at between 15,000 to 25,000 people, waiting. He spoke for two hours and eight minutes and the standing crowd responded with "polite applause."[1] Abe arose to address the somewhat tired and restless audience and to the surprise of all was back in his seat three minutes later.

Surrounded by thousands of graves of the fallen, Abe began, "Four score and seven years ago our fathers brought forth on this continent, a new nation, conceived in Liberty, and dedicated to the proposition that all men are created equal."[2]

With the authority of the president of the United States, Abe expressed his determination to reclaim the broken Union and to free all slaves because "all men were created equal."[3] He believed he was doing God's will. He would not bend on these principles nor would he let America forget that the Founding Fathers were far from foolish men for proclaiming that all men were created equal as many proslavery politicians claimed.

On that cold gray November day Abe continued, "Now we are engaged in a great civil war, testing whether this nation, or any nation so conceived and so dedicated, can long endure."[4]

Abe dedicated the battlefield to the brave men whose lives had ended here and whose blood had been spilt in battles throughout the land. But then he reminded the people what the thousands of brave souls died for reasons that could not be forgotten. It was now up to the living to unify the states again and free all men—no matter their color.

Then Abe sat down. The crowd was surprised when he ended his speech so suddenly. They expected that he would speak much longer. But his powerful message left them with a sense that their president fully understood the magnitude of the conflict and that he and he alone could guide them through it.

Abe doubted his speech's effectiveness and said to his aid, Ward Hill Lamon, "Lamon, that speech won't scour! It is a flat failure, and the people are disappointed."[5] Abe was wrong. His short Gettysburg Address has become the most celebrated speech in American history.

Armed with his newfound conviction that it was God's will that the slaves be freed, Abe was determined to complete the unthinkable and utilize the war itself to end slavery. And as the critics correctly pointed out, he had successfully used his Gettysburg Address to ensure equality as a main issue to be dealt with. The support from the rest of the nation confirmed his success in declaring racial equality as a new objective in the war.

Abe took advantage of his strong position to press the **Republican platform** to include a Constitutional amendment to end slavery in every state. The proposal was greeted with resounding applause and support. This opened the door for Abe to begin the process of gathering the support he needed for the Thirteenth Amendment to the Constitution.

Republican Platform: The Republican platform is the Republican Party's declaration of their opinions, motives, and planned actions.

The arrival of 1864 brought the buzz of anticipation for the November presidential election. No president since Andrew Jackson had been reelected, some thirty years earlier. But Abe wanted to complete the mission he had started. He told a friend, "It is not a good idea to change horses mid stream."[6]

As the months rolled on, candidates emerged to oppose Abe. But again he did nothing to promote himself. Instead, he focused his attention on the pressing matters of war and let the election process run its course.

Remarkably, his 1863 speeches and newspaper messages together with some key Union victories reversed the tide of dissatisfaction with him and his presidency. At the

Republican National Convention in June 1864, Abe was clearly the front runner. But that didn't guarantee that he would win against the Democratic candidate. He worried that defeat would end all that he had hoped to gain in preserving the Union and the Constitution.

He said, "I confess that I desire to be re-elected. [I want] to finish this job of putting down the rebellion, and restoring peace and prosperity to the country."[7]

As important as his re-election was, he couldn't and wouldn't devote much of his time to running against the Democratic Party's candidate. "I cannot run the political machine," he said, "I have enough on my hands without *that*. It is the *people's* business."[8] During that year he participated in none of the hundreds of pro-Lincoln campaigns. And he made very few public appearances in 1864.

Though he was the resounding choice for the Republican ticket, Abe faced mounting opposition from the Democrats who wanted to compromise with the South to end the bloodshed with their "Peace at Any Price" campaign.[9] But compromise meant stepping back from freeing the slaves and a less-than-complete reunification of the States, neither of which Abe would do.

Abe Lincoln was re-elected to serve four more years as president of the United States. The night of the re-election, after he retired to his room, Ward Hill Lamon quietly arrived outside the president's door with blankets, pistols, and bowie knives, and there he slept in mounting fear that many, more than ever, sought to take Abe's life.

***

Ever since he was a young man, Abe had always wanted to see slavery end in America. But his initial proclamation ended slavery only in the Southern rebelling states. He

took it no further at the time because he did not want to create even more division across the nation. Now with the support of the people he began his plan to end slavery in every state. He worked tirelessly and skillfully with the opposing Democrats in Congress for the **ratification** of a Thirteenth Amendment to the United States Constitution that would officially end slavery.

> **Ratification:** In the United States, amendments to the Constitution require the ratification or agreement of state legislatures.

On January 31, 1865, amid a storm of cheers, Abe watched as Congress, under his guidance, proposed to the state legislatures that the Thirteenth Amendment be ratified.[10]

With guarded elation, he observed over the months until his assassination in April how one by one, beginning with his own home state of Illinois, twenty-seven of the thirty-six states—the needed **three fourths majority**—ratified the new Amendment to end slavery forever in this nation.

> **Three Fourths Majority:** Our Constitution requires a three-fourths majority vote to amend or change the Constitution itself. Three-fourths of all states must ratify, or approve an amendment.

The other states eventually ratified the Amendment. Mississippi—the last state—officially ratified the amendment in 2013. At the news of the Amendment's passing, blacks assembled in large groups, clapping and singing over their new freedom.

From the White House Abe pronounced the amendment, "a great moral victory"[11] and it was.

***

Abe was quite sick as Inauguration Day approached. He admitted to his long time friend, Joshua Speed, "I am very unwell. . . . My feet and hands are always cold—I suppose I ought to be in bed."[12]

On March 4th, Abe climbed into the carriage and rode down Pennsylvania Avenue to the Capitol where he would give his second inaugural address and be sworn in for four more years. Waving crowds and playing bands lined the muddy streets. Inauguration Day was again wet, cold, windy, and gray.

This inauguration was very different from the first. Most of the estimated forty thousand people present carried the hurt of a lost loved one in their hearts. There were many more black faces in the crowd than at any other inauguration. They wanted to hear the words of their liberator. And for the first time, they were free to attend.

Thousands of soldiers were present as well, most from the some forty hospitals in the Washington area. Many were sad and pain-ridden amputees. Others bore disfigured faces and heads from bullets or shrapnel. But hope still lingered that the war was near its end.

Still others bore a boiling hatred and resentment for the North and especially for Abe Lincoln. They believed he had inflicted a terrible injustice on the South. One such believer stood in the crowd some thirty-five feet away from Abe as he gave the greatest sermon of his presidency. John Wilkes Booth looked intently at Abe as his mind conjured up his delusional plans to accomplish what so many had failed to do. He wanted Abe dead.

Abe approached the podium when, to everyone's surprise, the clouds suddenly parted and the brilliant warm sunlight shone on him and the large crowd. Abe felt that the sunburst was a sign from God, accepting the work of His humble and unwavering servant who unknowingly had only forty-two more days to live.

Abe's address consisted of 703 words, the second shortest inaugural address to be given. George Washington's was the shortest when no tradition was yet in place for newly elected presidents.

Unlike most political speeches, which are organized and reviewed by a team of speech writers, Abe developed his alone. He no doubt wrote them with an open Bible and frequent prayer asking his trusted God for guidance.

Abe began his address with an introduction and a very brief overview of the past four years' events. Neither the North or South wanted war, but war still came. And each side prayed for the failure of the other.

Abe said, "It may seem strange that any man should dare to ask a just God's assistance in wringing their bread from the sweat of other men's faces. . . . The prayers of both could not be answered; that of neither has been answered fully."[13]

Unexpectedly to everyone, he was ready to close and would do it by expressing words of kindness, and devotion. "Fondly do we hope—fervently do we pray—that this mighty scourge of war may speedily pass away."[14]

Then, with the warmth of a caring parent, he concluded, "With malice toward none; with charity for all; with firmness in the right, as God gives us to see the right, let us strive on to finish the work we are in; to bind up the nation's wounds, to care for him who shall have borne the battle, and for his widow, and the orphan—to do all which may achieve and cherish a just, and a lasting peace, among ourselves, and with all nations.[15]

In seven minutes, even as people were still arriving, the speech was over. He bowed solemnly to the applauding crowd and turned to the Supreme Court Chief Justice, Salmon Chase, to be sworn in as president.

Chapter Eleven

"Now He Belongs to the Ages"[1]

On Good Friday, April 14, 1865, Abe began his final day in mortality with breakfast in company of Mary and their oldest son, Captain Robert Todd Lincoln. Robert had just arrived from his military service as an aid for General Ulysses S. Grant at Appomattox, Virginia. The Lincolns were joyful to see their son again and were relieved that he had escaped harm. Robert was able to inform his father on many details of General Robert E. Lee's surrender to General Grant. Robert spent that crucial day on the porch of the Appomattox farmhouse in which Grant and Lee met for the surrender of the Confederate Army.

Elizabeth Keckley, Mary's official dressmaker, observed, "[Lincoln's] face was more cheerful than I had seen it for a long while."[2]

Abe was in high spirits. This Good Friday was certainly one of the happiest days of his presidency.

Later that morning, he held his final cabinet meeting, although no one dreamed that it would be their last. General Grant had been invited to report on the surrender at Appomattox.

Abe's Secretary of War, Edwin Stanton, said that Abe "spoke very kindly of General Lee and others of the Confederacy," exhibiting "in marked degree the kindness and humanity of his disposition, and the tender and forgiving spirit that so eminently distinguished him."[3]

They spent much of their meeting speaking of their concern and plans for the well-being of the citizens in the now vanquished South. Such sentiments for their former enemies by his cabinet reflected that Abe's plan for forgiveness and charity was taking hold.

That evening when the Lincolns arrived at Ford's Theater, the play was well into the first act. Anxious spectators kept looking expectantly up at the president's theater box above the stage for their arrival. The moment they entered the theater, actors paused and the orchestra began playing the presidential theme song, "Hail to the Chief." The audience leaped to their feet in loud applause and cheering for their victorious president.

One spectator remembered, "The President stepped to the box rail and acknowledged the applause with dignified bows and never-to-be-forgotten smiles."[4]

Abe sat by his wife Mary for over an hour, entertained by the performance and clearly enjoying each other's company. Mary nestled close to her husband and whispered, noting their guests, the Rathbones who shared their private theater box, "What will [they] think of my hanging on to you so?"

Abe smiled at his wife. "[They] won't think any thing about it."[5]

The guard who was stationed with the footman at the presidential box's rear entrance momentarily left his post, leaving the footman alone to guard the entrance.

At about 10:12 p.m., the flawlessly dressed John Wilkes Booth confidently walked up to the footman, presented him his card and chatted briefly with him. Everyone in Washington, including the Lincolns, knew the famous actor with his dashing good looks. After a few moments, Booth calmly said that he would like to enter the presidential box. Without any hesitation, the footman allowed the famous actor, who had starred many times in Ford's Theater, to enter.

Booth entered silently and stood behind the Lincolns and their guests. Knowing the play by heart, Booth watched as two actors exited, leaving only one actor on the stage, exactly as scripted. He was thrilled that his plot was working perfectly. His moment for fame and glory had arrived, and he wanted as much of the stage as possible for himself.

Booth waited patiently for the lone actor's upcoming line, which always brought a wave of laughter. Just as the audience burst into an uproarious laugh, Booth raised his pistol two feet from the president and fired. A single bullet penetrated the back of President Lincoln's head.

Abe slumped unconscious in his chair, as if asleep. Blood soaked his white collared shirt and pooled around his neck. The young Major Rathbone seated at the side of the Lincolns lunged toward the assassin, but Booth sliced Rathbone from the elbow to nearly the shoulder with his sharpened hunting knife. The deep wound bled profusely. Booth shoved him aside and vaulted over the rail of the box onto the stage.

The audience was confused. Were they being treated to an unscripted surprise? The heavy laughter had muffled the sound of the gunshot, and the familiar sight of John

Wilkes Booth leaping to the stage was not unexpected. He often had dramatic leaping entrances from heights of ten to twelve feet. But Booth's relished leap in front of the startled audience did not turn out as planned. His spur caught on one of the draped flags over the box railing, causing an awkward landing. His triumphant leap to the stage resulted in a broken leg.

In spite of the pain in his leg, Booth yelled, "*Sic semper tyrannis*" ("Thus always to tyrants"—the motto of the state of Virginia). He raised his knife, still slick with Rathbone's blood. "The South is avenged!"

At that moment Mary Lincoln screamed, "They have shot the president! They have shot the president!" Blue gray smoke from the gunshot rose from the presidential box.[6]

The audience gasped. Ladies screamed. This was no act! Their entertaining evening had just turned into one of the most tragic moments in American history.

Booth hobbled to the alley and his waiting horse. The confusion behind him allowed him to easily escape undetected out of the city and into the dark night.

Twelve days later, John Wilkes Booth, the revered actor, was hunted down and unceremoniously shot and killed while hiding in a barn. The previous twelve days allowed Booth to live long enough to realize that the South did not regard his assassination of President Lincoln as a heroic act. They were devastated. The Southern leaders saw Abe's compassion and kindness as the one great source of safety to which they could cling.

John Wilkes Booth would become a hero to no one.

***

With near pandemonium throughout the theater and

into the street, the unconscious president was hastily carried out of the theater through the thronging and angry crowd and across the street to the Peterson house where he was laid on a bed. There he would labor with strained and uneven breathing until the next morning.

April 15, at 7:22 a.m., the doctors said, "It is all over! The President is no more!"[7] President Abraham Lincoln was dead.

Everyone in the room fell silent, except for his son Robert who wept. How could such a great man who had done so much for this country be—gone?

Abe's Secretary of War, Edwin Stanton, asked a minister and close friend of Abe's, Dr. Gurley, to pray. Then with tears streaming down his cheeks, Stanton stood at the foot of the bed. This giant of a man in his own right paid a solemn salute to the first president to be assassinated in office. He lifted his hat in a reverent salute and said mournfully, "Now he belongs to the ages."[8]

***

Abraham Lincoln does belong to the ages. Times have changed a lot since he lived a century and half ago, but the qualities that define a hero have never changed. The powers he used in saving our nation and freeing the blacks are the same abilities that all of us can have—determination, respect, courage, and love.

As a boy Abe had no pen or paper. He used coals from the fire to practice his writing on a shovel or a stick to write in the snow. When he had no money to attend law school, he studied hard and taught himself to be a lawyer. When faced with the daunting goal to move from poverty to president of the United States, he thought of an ingenious plan and worked his plan for six years until his election. When faced with the many challenges of Civil War and slavery, he used his ingenuity, his faith, and his determination to turn these hardships into a lasting benefit to all. Nothing was impossible to him. This everyday hero decided to be the best he could be and by so doing he affected his family, his town, his country, and finally the world.

Endnotes

CHAPTER ONE: "THAR'S SUTHIN' PECULIARSOME 'BOUT ABE"

1. Sandburg, *Abraham Lincoln*, 26
2. Kunhardt, Kunhardt, and Kunhardt, *Lincoln: An Illustrated Biography*, 38
3. Kunhardt, Kunhardt, and Kunhardt, *Lincoln: An Illustrated Biography*, 38
4. Donald, *Lincoln*, 26–28
5. Kunhardt, Kunhardt, and Kunhardt, *Lincoln: An Illustrated Biography*, 12
6. Donald, *Lincoln*, 28
7. Ibid., 29
8. Ibid., 30
9. Ibid., 30
10. Sandburg, *Abraham Lincoln*, 26
11. Ibid.
12. Ibid.
13. Kunhardt, Kunhardt, and Kunhardt, *Lincoln: An Illustrated Biography*, 39
14. Atkinson, *The Boyhood of Lincoln*, 12
15. Ibid.
16. Donald, *Lincoln*, 32
17. Sandburg, *Abraham Lincoln*, 26
18. Ibid.
19. Ibid., 51

CHAPTER TWO: A PIECE OF FLOATING DRIFTWOOD

1. Ostendorf, *Abraham Lincoln: The Boy, The Man*, 55
2. Ibid.
3. Ibid.
4. Donald, *Lincoln*, 38
5. Sandburg, *Abraham Lincoln*, 24
6. Ibid., 25
7. Ibid.
8. Ibid.
9. Ibid.
10. Ibid.
11. Ibid.
12. Ibid.
13. Sandburg, *Abraham Lincoln*, 302
14. Osgood, *Funny Letters from Famous People*
15. Donald, *Lincoln*, 41
16. Kunhardt, Kunhardt, and Kunhardt, *Lincoln: An Illustrated Biography*, 38
17. Minor, "Lincoln the Lover," *The Atlantic Monthly*, (January, 1929), http://www.theatlantic.com/magazine/archive/1929/01/lincoln-the-lover/304445/..
18. Sandburg, *Abraham Lincoln*, 33

CHAPTER THREE: "SOME LEGAL RIGHTS ARE MORAL WRONGS."

1. Lamon, *Recollections of Abraham Lincoln: 1847–1865*, 222
2. Thomas, *Lincoln's New Salem*, 114.
3. Lamon, *Recollections of Abraham Lincoln: 1847–1865*, 222

CHAPTER FOUR: MARY TODD

1. Donald, *Lincoln*, 85
2. Ibid., 87
3. Ibid., 88
4. Ibid.
5. Ibid., 91
6. Ibid., 93

7. Oates, *Abraham Lincoln*, 44
8. Kunhardt, Kunhardt, and Kunhardt, *Lincoln: An Illustrated Biography*, 90
9. Donald, *Lincoln*, 100
10. Phillips, *Lincoln on Leadership*, 18
11. Gross, *The Wit and Wisdom of Abraham Lincoln*, 9

CHAPTER FIVE: CONGRESSMAN LINCOLN

1. Sandburg, *Abraham Lincoln*, 84
2. Donald, *Lincoln*, 149
3. Fehrenbacher and Fehrenbacher, *Recollected Words of Abraham Lincoln*, 241
4. Miller, *Lincoln's Virtues*, 232
5. Ibid., 238
6. Donald, *Lincoln*, 206
7. Ibid.

CHAPTER SIX: WHAT WAS HE THINKING?

1. Miller, *Lincoln's Virtues*, 234
2. Ibid., 238
3. Ibid., 249
4. Ibid.
5. Andersen, *Abraham Lincoln: God's Humble Instrument*, 98 (italics in original)
6. Humes, *The Wit and Wisdom of Abraham Lincoln*, 73
7. Donald, *Lincoln*, 149
8. Wolf, *The Almost Chosen People*, 150
9. Andersen, *Abraham Lincoln: God's Humble Instrument*, 150
10. Ibid., 101–102
11. Miller, *Lincoln's Virtues*, 238
12. Ibid., 239
13. Ibid., 270 (italics in original)
14. Ibid.
15. Donald, *Lincoln*, 176
16. Ibid.

17. Ibid.
18. Miller, *Lincoln's Virtues*, 270

CHAPTER SEVEN: THE UNLIKELY PRESIDENT

1. Donald, *Lincoln*, 238
2. Ibid.
3. Ibid., 239
4. Ibid.
5. Ibid., 242
6. Ibid.
7. Ibid.
8. Ibid., 251
9. Ibid.
10. Ibid., 254
11. Ibid., 256
12. Kunhardt, Kunhardt, and Kunhardt, *Lincoln: An Illustrated Biography*, 133
13. Ibid.

CHAPTER EIGHT: OFF TO WASHINGTON

1. Ostendorf, *Abraham Lincoln: The Boy, The Man*, 104
2. Donald, *Lincoln*, 271
3. Ibid., 272
4. White Jr., *The Eloquent President*, 10
5. Ibid.
6. Ibid., 4
7. Ibid., 3
8. Ibid., 22
9. Ibid., 23
10. Ibid., 54 (italics in original)

CHAPTER NINE: I, ABRAHAM LINCOLN, DO SOLEMNLY SWEAR

1. Donald, *Lincoln*, 283
2. White Jr., *The Eloquent President*, 87 (italics in original)
3. Ibid., 62
4. Ibid., 92

5. Donald, *Lincoln*, 295
6. Hanchett, *Out of the Wilderness*, 33
7. Donald, *Lincoln*, 402
8. Thayer, *The Life and Letters of John Hay*, 76
9. White Jr., *The Eloquent President*, 168
10. Ibid., 170
11. Oates, *With Malice Toward None*, 340
12. Ibid.

CHAPTER TEN: A NEW BIRTH OF FREEDOM

1. White Jr., *The Eloquent President*, 242
2. Andersen, *Abraham Lincoln: God's Humble Instrument*, 268
3. Ibid.
4. White Jr., *The Eloquent President*, 223
5. Ibid., 234
6. Donald, *Lincoln*, 493
7. Ibid., 540
8. Ibid., 537 (italics in original)
9. Hill, *Abraham Lincoln: Man of God*, 299
10. Oates, *With Malice Toward None*, 405
11. Ibid.
12. Ibid., 409
13. White Jr., *The Eloquent President*, 290
14. Ibid., 293
15. Ibid., 301

CHAPTER ELEVEN: "NOW HE BELONGS TO THE AGES"

1. Donald, *Lincoln*, 599
2. Goodwin, *Team of Rivals*, 731
3. Ibid., 732
4. Donald, *Lincoln*, 595
5. Ibid.
6. Swanson, *Manhunt*, 19
7. Donald, *Lincoln*, 599
8. Ibid.

Sources

Andersen, Ron L. *Abraham Lincoln: God's Humble Instrument.* Salt Lake City, Utah: Millennial Mind Publishing, 2010.

Atkinson, Elenor. *The Boyhood of Lincoln.* New York: McClure Company, 1958.

Donald, David Herbert. *Lincoln.* New York: Touchstone, 1995.

Fehrenbacher, Don E., and Virginia Fehrenbacher. *Recollected Words of Abraham Lincoln.* Stanford, California: Stanford University Press, 1996

Goodwin, Doris Kearns. *Team of Rivals: The Political Genius of Abraham Lincoln.* New York: Simon & Schuster, 2006.

Gross, Anthony ed. *The Wit and Wisdom of Abraham Lincoln.* New York: Barnes Noble, 1994.

Hanchett, William. *Out of the Wilderness: The Life of Abraham Lincoln.* Champaign, Illinois: University of Illinois Press, 1994.

Hill, John Wesley. *Abraham Lincoln: Man of God.* (New York: G. P. Putnam's Sons, 1920.

Humes, James C. *The Wit and Wisdom of Abraham Lincoln: A Treasury of More Than 1000 Quotations and Anecdotes.* Toronto, Ontario, CA: HarperCollins Canada, 1996.

Kunhardt, Philip B. Jr., Philip Kunhardt III, Peter W. Kunhardt. *Lincoln, An Illustrated Biography.* New York: Alfred A. Knopf, 1992.

Lamon, Ward Hill. *Recollections of Abraham Lincoln: 1847–1865*. Lincoln, Nebraska: University of Nebraska Press, 1994.

Miller, William Lee. *Lincoln's Virtues: An Ethical Biography*. New York: Vintage Books, 2003

Minor, Wilma Frances. "Lincoln the Lover." *The Atlantic Monthly*, (January, 1929), http://www.theatlantic.com/magazine/archive/1929/01/lincoln-the-lover/304445/.

Oates, Stephen B. *Abraham Lincoln: the Man Behind the Myths*. New York: Harper & Row, 1984.

Oates, Stephen B. *With Malice Toward None: A Life of Abraham Lincoln*. New York: Harper & Row, 1977.

Osgood, Charles. *Funny Letters from Famous People*. New York: Broadway Books, 2003.

Ostendorf, Lloyd. *Abraham Lincoln: The Boy, the Man*. Springfield, Illinois: Phillip H. Wagner, 1962.

Phillips, Donald T. *Lincoln on Leadership: Executive Strategies for Tough Times*. New York: Warner Books, 1992.

Sandburg, Carl. *Abraham Lincoln: The Prairie Years and the War Years*. Pleasantville, New York: Readers Digest Association, 1954.

Swanson, James L. *Manhunt: the 12-Day Chase for Lincoln's Killer*. New York: William Morrow, 2006.

Thayer, William Roscoe. *The Life and Letters of John Hay*. Ithaca, New York: Cornell University Press, 1915.

Thomas, Benjamin P. *Lincoln's New Salem*. Carbondale, Illinois: Southern Illinois University Press, 1988.

White, Ronald C. Jr. *The Eloquent President: A Portrait of Lincoln through His Words*. New York: Random House, 2005

Wolf, William J. *The Almost Chosen People: A Study of the Religion of Abraham Lincoln*. Garden City, New York: Doubleday, 1959.

About the Author

Ron L. Andersen is the founder of the Lincoln Leadership Society and a dynamic and compelling public speaker on the remarkable life of Abraham Lincoln. He maintains a following of thousands of Lincoln admirers, and this is his third book on the subject of Abraham Lincoln. Ron also served for six years on the board of the largest young men's organization in the world, promoting integrity and faith in the lives of over 600,000 youth in nearly every country.

Ron is also a popular Lincoln lecturer, traveling the country speaking at various community forums. He is married to Kathleen Brown, and together they have five children and ten grandchildren.

About the Illustrator

As a young boy, Jay Fontano loved to watch cartoons and read comic strips in the newspaper. Now he works as an illustrator drawing funny pictures for T-shirts and illustrating books.

Jay and his wife have six children and enjoy spending time together camping, swimming, exploring, and having fun. They live near a creek close to the mountains with their dog, Nacho, and a small flock of chickens.

He still watches cartoons and reads comic strips.

0 26575 17895 1